Exploring What Jesus Says About Discipleship

A 30-day Devotional

Gwynedd Jones

First Edition 2019

Streetlamp Publishers

streetlamppublishers@gmail.com

ISBN: 978-0-9934165-6-9

Cover: rhysllwyd.com

"Lord, to whom shall we go?
You have the words (the message)
of eternal life."

Simon Peter, one of Jesus' first followers

(John 6:68 - AMPC)

Contents

Introduction

Following Jesus is the greatest privilege any individual can have in life. He loves unconditionally, brings clarity to why we exist, and gives a secure hope for the future - even into eternity. During His earthly ministry, Jesus went to great lengths to explain what it means to follow Him. Jesus hasn't changed, so what He said 2,000 years ago is as relevant today as it was then. What exactly did Jesus say about what it means to follow Him? Thankfully, His words have been recorded for us in the Gospels, which means that every individual who is serious about following Jesus today is given the opportunity to hear *for themselves* what He said regarding what it means to be His disciple.

The primary focus of this devotional is to look at what *Jesus* said about what it means to follow Him. There is no one better to learn from regarding what it means to be a disciple of Jesus, than Jesus Himself. He is the One who taught about discipleship in its purest form in the first instance. There is no doubt that Jesus was extremely successful in making disciples. He called twelve *ordinary* men to follow Him, and over a period of only three years He discipled them in such a way that not only were they able to continue His ministry, they actually multiplied it. As we acknowledge His success in making disciples, the least we can do therefore is to look at what *He* taught regarding what it means to be His disciple. It's as we hear what Jesus says that we begin to understand the principles, receive the wisdom, and hopefully have our eyes opened to the revelation of what it means to follow Him. That in turn helps us to be more effective in what God has called us to do for the increase of His Kingdom.

Introduction

So what does it mean to be a disciple of Jesus, and what is the purpose of discipleship? How do we know whether we're a true disciple or simply going through the motions? If we've received Jesus Christ as our personal Saviour, are we then okay to sit back until He returns? Where does the responsibility lie with regard to discipleship - the individual, the church, or both? By focusing on what Jesus says about discipleship, this 30-day devotional will hopefully bring clarity not only to these questions, but also to other questions we may have regarding the subject of being a follower of Jesus.

Throughout His earthly ministry Jesus said some challenging and controversial things, including some things about the subject of what it means to follow Him. We can be excused for thinking that sometimes it sounded as if He was actually trying to put people off following Him, rather than encouraging them to take the journey with Him! Hopefully, this book will help bring clarity to some of these areas as well; with the hope that the follower will experience the freedom and grace Jesus wants every individual to enjoy.

If we're serious about following Jesus, then this devotional will benefit us. It's written to help bring clarity, understanding, and encouragement to every person who is following the One who promises abundant Life (John 10:10). Because the journey is unique to every individual, neither this book, nor any other book can answer every question we may have regarding what it means to follow Jesus. However, by focusing on a number of the foundational principles regarding what Jesus says about discipleship, my hope is that this devotional will be a real help in one way or another to those who are walking with Him.

Introduction

It's by hearing what *Jesus* has to say about discipleship that we're able to go to the very heart of understanding what it means to be His disciple. It's as we hear *His* voice that we're able to say, together with one of His first disciples, *"Lord, to whom shall we go? You have words of eternal life. We have believed and have come to know that You are the Holy One of God".* (Simon Peter - John 6:68-69). Enjoy the journey!

(The short italicised section at the end of each day's devotion is a prayer as well as a declaration of faith. Whenever possible, it should be spoken out aloud).

The Call To Follow

Day 1

Have You Heard His Voice?

"Come, follow me...."
Jesus - Matthew 4:19 (NLT)

Inviting people to follow Him was a central and fundamental part of Jesus' ministry. It was one of the first things He did at the very start of His public ministry, which shows the value He placed on it. Jesus would not be Jesus if He didn't call men (and women) to follow Him.

I wonder how many people heard Jesus' invitation to *"Come, follow me"*?[1.] We know Andrew and his brother Peter did because it's recorded how they left their fishing nets so they could follow Him[2]. John and his brother James did the same - they left their nets, their boat, as well as their father on the shore of the Sea of Galilee in response to Jesus' call[3]. Phillip was another one[4], as was Levi (also known as Matthew), the tax collector[5]. These men were prepared to leave everything they had, for someone they didn't yet know, because they had glimpsed in Jesus a treasure that was far greater than what they were leaving behind[6].

Many responded positively to Jesus' invitation, but sadly there were many who didn't. A wealthy and influential young man met Jesus one day as He was travelling, and though he was eager to follow Jesus we're told he declined the invitation when Jesus explained to him he would need to change his priorities[7]. There were others who started to follow Him but as they heard Jesus' claims about Himself, they got offended and turned back[8]. Undoubtedly, these are some of the saddest accounts we can read about in Jesus' ministry. These people had been drawn to Jesus because they saw in Him something that was unique and compelling, with His words somehow speaking to their deepest needs. There would even have been a time when they had looked directly into the eyes of God Himself, in the person of Jesus Christ, yet they turned away from following Him, thinking they would find a greater and more meaningful purpose elsewhere.

What about you? Have *you* heard His voice? Is there something within you that draws you to want to know more about this person Jesus Christ? Are you attracted and captivated by the things He says? If you are, then Jesus is saying the same thing to you now as He did to Andrew, Peter, and John all those years ago when He said *'Come, follow me'*. The desire you have to know more about this person Jesus Christ is His invitation for you to follow Him. If you haven't already done so, don't leave it any longer before you say to Him *'Yes, I will'*. It's as we make this choice that we come to know that Jesus is the One who has the words of eternal life[9]. Everything starts however with responding to the royal invitation to *'Come, follow me....'*.

"Jesus, I acknowledge this deep sense of calling within me that attracts me to You. I don't fully comprehend it Lord, but I know enough to understand that it's Your invitation for me to follow You. I say a wholehearted 'yes' to You today Lord - I choose to follow You with all my heart and I thank You for this privileged invitation. In Jesus' Name. Amen"

Day 2

He Is The Teacher; We Are The Pupils

"Accept my teaching. Learn from me.
I am gentle and humble in spirit...."
Jesus - Matthew 11:29 (ERV)

A disciple is a 'learner'. A learner is simply someone who is seeking to gain knowledge or skills they don't currently possess. For the disciple of Jesus, the source they are looking to in order to gain this knowledge is Jesus Himself. This is remarkable, because it means they are effectively looking to learn from the One who is the Wisdom that Solomon talks about in the Book of Proverbs[1]. They are looking to learn from the One who speaks the words of God Himself[2]; as well as to the One the Old Testament writes about[3]. This Jesus is the One whose words carry the very life of God within them[4], so the invitation to *'accept my teaching and learn from me'*[5] carries with it a solemnity we would be foolish to ignore. What is even more remarkable is this invitation goes out to the *ignorant and naive*[6]. The One who has the words of eternal life[7] invites *us* to learn from Him - what a privilege!

True disciples of Jesus do not limit themselves to simply learning 'information' from Him. A true disciple learns from Jesus, *then applies the knowledge they have gained so that it becomes their lifestyle*[8]. By applying what they are learning from their Teacher, the follower eventually starts to *imitate* the One who is teaching them, thus demonstrating the life, qualities, and characteristics of the One they are following[9].

9

Jesus is not looking for people who simply want to increase their 'head knowledge', because He knows that knowledge alone can make people proud[10]. Jesus is actually looking for people who want a relationship with Him. He's looking for people who are willing to surrender to His love so that He can form His image within them, enabling them to accurately represent Him to the world around them. This means therefore that the true disciple needs to surrender their *heart*, as well as their *head* to the teachings of Jesus. Naturally, 'head knowledge' does increase as we follow Jesus, but in the absence of surrendering our hearts so that we can be changed by the Holy Spirit from within, having head knowledge alone will not accomplish the perfect will of God in our lives[11].

Jesus' ministry was only three years long, which is extremely short for someone who has changed the course of world history. What is significant however is that Jesus invested a substantial amount of this time discipling twelve (ordinary) men so that His ministry would continue after His ascension. This speaks volumes regarding the value Jesus places on discipleship. The more we are prepared to invest in our relationship with Jesus, the more He will reveal Himself to us[12]. As we do this, His image will be formed within us[13] so that we will not only be called to *represent* Him to the world around us[14]; we will also be called to *reproduce* Him to a world that is seeking the true meaning and purpose of its existence[15].

"Father, thank You for the privilege of being invited to follow You. You have the words of eternal life Lord, and I give you all of my heart so that I can grow in my relationship with You, and in the process be changed by You. I recognise I can only find the abundant life of freedom and peace that You promise by giving my all to You Lord, which I now do. Thank You for Your grace and kindness to me. In Jesus' Name I pray. Amen"

Convert, or Disciple?

"From the time of John until now, people try hard to break into the kingdom of heaven. And strong people take hold of it."
Jesus - Matthew 11:12 (WE)

In learning what it means to follow Jesus, it's important to understand the difference between a *convert* and a *disciple*. In it's simplest form, a 'convert' is someone who hears the Gospel, responds positively to its message by placing faith in Jesus Christ for their salvation, but then fails to grow spiritually beyond that point[1]. A disciple on the other hand is someone who continues to grow *spiritually* beyond their conversion, so that the nature and character of Christ becomes more and more evident in their lives, enabling them to *'walk just like Jesus did'*[2].

The convert who fails to embrace *discipleship* will not fully mature into the person God has designed them to be. This is because the new birth they have experienced at the core of their being (where the miracle of spiritual transformation takes place) is denied the opportunity to change them with respect to the way they think, feel, and act. This means they will continue to live their lives in generally the same way they did prior to their conversion, except for possibly a few small changes here and there. The 'flesh' is still in control of their lives, because they have failed to allow the Word of God (the Bible) to re-shape their thinking and decision-making - something that can only come about as a result of discipleship.

God's plan for every Christian is that through a deepening relationship with Him, the character of Christ is formed within them so that they become the image of Christ here on earth, displaying His likeness to those around them[3]. Having the image of Christ formed within means the individual is able to do the things Jesus did when He was here on earth[4]. *A failure to embrace discipleship* therefore means not only will the individual fall drastically short of this, but there is also the real danger they will actually become a negative witness for Christ rather than the positive one God has intended. Because they are still governed by their flesh rather than being led by the Spirit[5], the convert will continue to display the 'old fruit' of gossip, backbiting, coarse or sexually suggestive humour, unforgiveness etc.[6]. This can lead to (justifiably) being called 'hypocrites' by some, because their *confession* of being followers of Christ is contradicted by the reality of their words, actions, and wrong attitudes.

Today's devotion is not about 'bashing' converts, because each and every convert is highly valued by God and individually celebrated in Heaven[7]. Rather, today is about *advocating discipleship*, because it is by understanding how much is at stake for us personally, as well as for the Gospel of Jesus Christ, that we are able to make the certain and intentional decision to fully embrace discipleship as we walk with Jesus. Know that you are loved by God whether you are a convert or a disciple, but take a few moments to reflect on whether now is the time to fully embrace what Jesus is offering you - a life of intimacy and victory that can only be truly realised by committing to follow Him *as a disciple*.

"Father, I am so grateful to You for saving me. Thank You for everything You have done for me Lord, and I make the decision today Lord Jesus, to settle for nothing less than following You as a true disciple. I know that as I make this choice, Heaven hears my cry and is released to act on my behalf, giving me the strength, the protection, and the guidance I need to remain faithful to what You have called me into. In Jesus' Name I pray this. Amen"

The Call To Discipleship

Making God's Kingdom Our First Priority

*"Seek the Kingdom of God above all else, and live righteously,
and he will give you everything you need."*
Jesus - Matthew 6:33 (NLT)

Jesus will never force anyone to follow Him - He always gives the individual a freedom to choose whether they want to come into a relationship with Him or not. Even when people make the wrong choice by deciding not to follow Him, He gives them the freedom to make that wrong choice[1]. However, what Jesus *does do* is help people understand what the consequences of their choice will be, thereby giving them the opportunity to make the right choice in the first instance.

A common barrier to fully committing to Jesus is money, which is one reason He taught so much on the subject. He taught on the dangers of money[2]; how money can deceive us[3] (because it gives us a false sense of purpose and security); as well as how trusting God with our money is the doorway into the *'true riches'* - the revelation of the full Gospel[4].

In today's headline verse, Jesus makes an amazing promise to those who are willing to put Him first in their lives. He says that when we choose to *'seek the Kingdom of God above all else'[5]*; all our needs will be met. He's saying that if our life's priority is to seek Him and His way of doing things (*'live righteously'*), then God will take care of all the material needs we have[6]. Jesus' confidence in making this promise is based on the *spiritual law* that comes into effect once we make the commitment to give everything over to following Him - a spiritual law that ensures all our needs are met by Heaven.

Unfortunately, we often get this the wrong way round by focusing on provision first, Kingdom of God second. It's not necessarily that we're spending all our energy on gaining worldly wealth - it's simply that we're so focused on making sure our daily needs are met that our relationship with Jesus takes second place. Jesus is telling us to make sure our priorities are right. Once we do, Heaven will provide for our needs because God already knows we need these things[7]. Notice there is no 'exclusion clause' or 'small print' attached to this promise - Jesus sets out the terms and conditions very clearly - *'make God first in every area of your life and He will provide for you'*.

When developing our relationship with Jesus becomes our top priority, we are positioning ourselves to be provided for in a far better way than we could ever provide for ourselves. In addition, we are giving God the opportunity to display His generosity. He is a generous Father who wants to lavish His children with good things, and by choosing to give His Kingdom first priority in our lives we're giving Him a freedom to display His goodness. Choosing to *seek His Kingdom and His righteousness* as our main priority is a *fundamental issue*, because it ushers us into the fullness of what He has in store for us. By accepting His invitation to put Him first, what we will find is that His provision will surpass all our expectations![8]

"Father, You know the fears and insecurities I have in this area of provision, but I want to learn how to trust You Lord. I do believe Your promises of provision, and so I make the choice to seek first Your Kingdom and Your righteousness, and leave the care of my provision with You. In Jesus' Name I pray this. Amen"

Day 5

Dying, So We Can Live

"If any of you wants to be my follower, you must give up your own way,
take up your cross daily, and follow me."
Jesus - Luke 9:23 (NLT)

When Jesus gave an invitation for people to follow Him, He always made sure they knew what they were letting themselves in for. In today's headline verse, He says they need to *'give up their own way'* and *'take up their cross daily'*. Jesus is simply saying we need to surrender our lives to Him completely and unequivocally - we need to give up our own dreams, our own ambitions, and any plans we may have - so that we can find the life He has for us[1]. It's only as we *let go of ourselves*, that we're able to *take hold of Him* and the future He has planned for us[2].

When a trapeze artist goes through their routine, there is a moment when they have to *let go* of one high bar in order to *take hold* of the next one. If they don't let go, they will keep on swinging back and forth until they eventually stop. For the Christian to fully enter into all that God has for them, they will need at some point to *let go* of their own dreams, plans, and personal desires, in order to *take hold* of the future that Jesus has for them. It's not an easy thing to do however because all sorts of reasons as to why we *shouldn't* 'let go' will come to us. But just like the trapeze artist, until we make the decision to let go of the old we will never experience the thrill of taking hold of the new. It's a sacred moment for the Christian when they make that choice, because it's a decision that is made at a *heart level* - the deepest, most intimate place of their being. It is there that

17

we say to the Lord Jesus, *'I'm letting go of myself, so I can take hold of You, and everything You've got for me'*.

Once we've done this, we can then start to *'take up our cross daily'* and follow Him. This is the daily process of crucifying our flesh so that the new nature we've been given through the new birth is allowed to dominate our personality (our soul). If we're prepared to give God's will (what He says in His Word) *daily* preference in our lives, we're effectively 'crucifying' our flesh (the old nature) by not allowing it to dictate to us how we choose to live our lives. By consistently obeying the Shepherd's voice[3] in preference to our own, we're allowing the Holy Spirit to form the image of Christ within us[4], which over time brings us the life, peace, and joy that God wants us to experience.

Jesus says *'whoever loses his life for My sake will find it'*[5]. He is encouraging us to 'lose' our old life so that through a relationship with Him, we can find the new life He has for us. If you haven't already let go of yourself in order to follow Jesus, I would strongly encourage you to take that step today. Until you do, it will be impossible to take hold of everything God has got for you[6].

"Father, I hear Your voice inviting me to let go of myself, so I can take hold of You. I take this opportunity now Lord to declare that I'm giving up all of my hopes, my plans, and my desires, so that I can fully embrace You, and all that You have for me. I do this in the precious Name of Jesus. Amen"

Following Jesus Today

"If you continue in My word, then you are truly disciples of Mine;"
Jesus - John 8:31b

When the first disciples heard Jesus' call to *'Come, follow Me'[1]*, they had a *physical* Jesus to follow. They were able to see where He was going and what He was doing, as well as hear with their ears what He was saying. Have you ever wondered how today's disciple is meant to follow Jesus, considering He is no longer physically here in the same way He was for the first disciples?

On the eve of His crucifixion, the disciples became troubled when Jesus told them He would be leaving them and *'going to the Father'[2]*. Knowing they were anxious about it, Jesus explained that even though His time to leave had come, it would not be long before they would see Him again[3]. He went on to say they would actually benefit as a result of Him going to the Father, because the Holy Spirit would be given to them[4]. He wasn't abandoning them, because He (and the Father) would soon be back with them[5], this time not *physically*, but *in the Person of the Holy Spirit[6]*. He would not only be *with* them when He came back, but also *in* them[7]. Jesus kept this promise because the Holy Spirit was given to His followers after His resurrection and ascension[8]. What we then see in the Book of Acts is that the disciples continued to follow Jesus, not the *physical* Jesus they had previously known, but the *spiritual* Jesus in the Person of the Holy Spirit[9].

It is the same for today's believer. We don't have Jesus' physical presence to follow, but we do have Him spiritually present in our lives - in the Person of the Holy Spirit. *Hearing the voice of the Holy Spirit talk to us through His Word (the Bible), and then being obedient to follow what He's saying is how the Christian follows Jesus today.*

By giving those who put their faith in Jesus Christ the Holy Spirit, God not only gives us the honour of knowing Him at a personal level[10], He also gives us the privilege of being able to hear His voice. If we ask and are then prepared to listen, the Holy Spirit will speak to us - not necessarily in an audible voice (though this does happen) - but spiritually, within our hearts. It's as we hear and then choose to be obedient to His voice that we grow in our relationship with Him and so become true followers[11]. The primary way we will hear the Shepherd[12] speak to us is through the Bible, which is why we're told the Word has a voice[13]. It's as we go into the Word of Truth[14] that the Holy Spirit will *'lead us into all truth'*[15], revealing Jesus to us[16], because Jesus is the Truth[17].

Make a decision today that you're not going to assume nor try to guess where Jesus is leading you, but that you are determined to hear His voice so you can have confidence as you follow. Commit to hearing Him as you read the Bible so that your relationship with Him can grow, and then choose to be obedient so He can take you into the plans He has for you, plans that *'give you a future and a hope'*[18].

"Father, please teach me to hear Your voice from Your Word. Help me to be sensitive to Your Spirit as I read the Bible, and obedient to Your prompting as You speak to me. I thank You Lord for the privilege of knowing You, and being called by You. I pray this in the Name of Jesus. Amen"

The Old Testament

"Every teacher of the law who has become a disciple in the kingdom of heaven is like the owner of a house. He brings new treasures out of his storeroom as well as old ones."
Jesus - Matthew 13:52 (NIrV)

After His resurrection, Jesus was walking with two of His followers on the road to Emmaus, but they were kept from recognising Him[1]. As they walked together He took them through the writings of Moses and the prophets (the Old Testament); explaining to them what the scriptures said about Him[2]. He said the same thing to a wider group of His followers a little later - explaining that what Moses, the prophets, and the psalmists had written was about Him[3].

It wasn't the first time Jesus had said the Old Testament scriptures were written about Him. During His ministry He reproached some Jews for thinking that by studying the scriptures they would find eternal life, when what they actually needed to do was to come to the One the scriptures were written about. He was the One who would give them eternal life[4], and told them *"If you really believed Moses, you would believe me, because he wrote about me"*[5].

As followers of Jesus, it's important for us to study the Old Testament. When we read the accounts of Biblical 'giants' such as Abraham, Joseph, and David (as examples), we're able to see 'types' of Jesus - individuals that help us understand some of the qualities of the Messiah. No one individual in the Old Testament was able to perfectly reflect the One who was to come, because in some way they were all flawed. Yet it's important for us to read about these individuals because as we study their lives and acknowledge their strengths, we're able to see the nature of the One who when He came, fully displayed these remarkable qualities.

By studying the Old Testament we also come to understand what Jesus has accomplished on our behalf. God made hundreds of promises to His people in the Old Testament, and Jesus makes it clear that He came to fulfil those promises[6]. In order to fully appreciate what Jesus has accomplished on our behalf, we have to first of all know what the promises are - which we're able to do by reading and studying the Old Testament ('the Law and the Prophets').

In today's headline verse, Jesus tells us that the follower who understands that the Old Testament speaks of Him, is like the owner of a house who is able to draw out *old*, as well as *new* treasures from their treasury (their heart)[7]. Though the truths may be regarded as 'old', they are still *treasure,* which therefore make them *extremely valuable*! As followers of Jesus Christ we cannot therefore afford to ignore the Old Testament. In it God reveals to us His master plan - His purpose for mankind, the promises He makes to His people, and how everything is perfectly revealed and fulfilled in the Person of Jesus Christ[8]. Make a commitment today to become the master of a household who brings out old, as well as new treasures from your heart, by reading, learning from, and studying the Old Testament.

"Father, I ask You to open the eyes of my heart so that I can see the precious treasures within Your Word. You are that Treasure Lord, so I ask You to show Yourself to me as I read and study the Old Testament. I pray this in the precious Name of Jesus. Amen"

Day 8

The Love Command

"But I am giving you a new command. You must love
each other, just as I have loved you."
Jesus - John 13:34 (CEV)

Jesus tells us we need to love God with all our heart, soul, and mind; and that we need to love those in the world (our 'neighbour') as ourselves[1]. He also tells us in today's headline verse that we need to love our fellow believers *as I have loved you*[2]. He's set the bar extremely high, because the type of love Jesus is talking about is *'agapáō love'*[3] - love in its highest and purest form.

If we think we can love at this level without God's help, then we are very much mistaken. Being able to love the way Jesus commands us to love is not within man's natural ability. This love is something we have to first of all be *given as a gift, and then out of the gift we've been given, we're able to love God and people in the way Jesus commands us to.* Because God is Love[4], when we choose to put our faith in Jesus Christ, God pours *His love* into our hearts by the Holy Spirit[5]. We cannot love God, our neighbour, or our fellow believer in line with Jesus' commandment until we have first of all *received* the love of God for ourselves through faith in Jesus Christ[6].

A miracle happens within our hearts when we put our faith in Christ. The Holy Spirit not only pours God's love into our hearts, He also removes the old spiritual heart we had - the one that had been hardened by sin. This is what the Bible refers to as the *circumcision of the heart* - the old sin nature that

23

surrounded our hearts is spiritually cut away, in order that we can receive the love of God as a gift. Moses understood the people's disobedience to God's Law was a *heart* issue, calling on them to have their hearts circumcised so they wouldn't continue in their rebellion[7]. Jeremiah did the same - he called on God's people to *'remove the foreskins of your heart'*[8] - telling them they needed to have the hard layer of sin that surrounded their hearts removed. This was so that God, through the New Covenant, could put His 'law' of love into their hearts[9]. The prophet Ezekiel said the same thing, though using different terminology when saying that God would remove the heart of stone from His people, and replace it with a heart of flesh[10].

The Old Testament promise of heart circumcision finds its fulfilment in Jesus Christ. As the individual turns in faith to Christ, their old sinful heart is circumcised (removed) - because of what Jesus has done on the cross[11]. God's promise that He would put His law (of love) into people's hearts through the New Covenant has now been realised in Jesus Christ. Jesus is the One who has brought in the New Covenant which Jeremiah spoke about[12]. This means that the follower of Christ is now able to *receive* God's love, as well as able to *give* God's love to those around them. God will never ask us to do anything He is not willing to underwrite, so by His Spirit, He has given us the power to love Him with all our heart; to love our neighbour as ourselves; and to love our fellow believer *as He loved us*. It all starts however with receiving Him, the One who is Love, through faith in Jesus Christ, and then living out of the love with which He has loved us[13].

"Father, I acknowledge that You are Love. Thank You for taking away my old, hardened, sinful nature and for pouring out Your love into my heart. Thank You for showing me how much You love me, and for enabling me to love You and those around me out of the love You have given me. In Jesus' Name I thank You. Amen"

24

Surrendering To Love

"So then, any of you who does not forsake (renounce, surrender claim to, give up, say good-bye to) all that he has cannot be My disciple."
Jesus - Luke 14:33 (AMPC)

Jesus' words in today's headline verse are challenging to say the least, and if we choose to ignore or resist them, we won't be able to experience everything He's promising us. So what does it mean to *'renounce, surrender claim to, give up, say good-bye to all that we have'?*[1.]

To start with, nobody has the ability (or right) to give a definitive answer regarding what Jesus' statement should look like in practice in someone else's life. Rather, it is up to the *individual* to understand a foundational principle regarding love, and then allow the Holy Spirit to guide and instruct them as to how Jesus' statement works out in practice for them. This is one of the privileges that comes with the New Covenant in Jesus - that as *individuals* we would come into a relationship with God[2] and be able to hear His voice[3], thus giving us the ability to discern *for ourselves* His will for our lives. It is out of our relationship with the Lord that we will know how to put into practice Jesus' words of surrendering everything to Him, not by other people instructing us[4].

The starting point to knowing how to follow Jesus' statement in practice is to first of all surrender our hearts *completely* and *unequivocally* to the love of God. The spiritual 'life' of every person flows out of their heart[5], and this 'life' can be either good or bad, depending on what's in the heart in the first instance[6].

Surrendering our hearts completely to the One who is Love[7] means it will be *love* that will be the 'life force' flowing from our hearts. Once surrendered, the thoughts, words, actions and choices flowing from that individual's heart will be aligned with the One who has become their Life Source - Love. *Love* then takes the responsibility of guiding each person as to how Jesus' words work out in practice for them.

A complete surrender to the love of God will cost us everything, because surrendering to Love means we are no longer in control of our own destiny - love is. Love is constantly looking to bless others before 'itself'[8], so we will lose the right to put ourselves at the centre. If we're going to find the abundant life Jesus is offering us[9], there is no other way than to surrender and allow the love of God to flood our hearts completely. It is somewhat of a paradox that it is by surrendering ourselves to become *slaves (of righteousness)*[10] that we find true freedom[11]. Surrender yourself today - utterly, completely, and wholeheartedly to the One who is Love, and allow love to be your Master.

"Father, thank You for pouring Yourself into my heart. I give You full control Lord, and declare before Heaven today that I surrender my heart completely to You - the One who is Love. Use me Lord as Your vessel to reach others with Your Love. For Your glory, and in the Name of Jesus I ask this. Amen"

Day 10

Swim Upstream

"But to you who are willing to listen, I say, love your enemies!
Do good to those who hate you."
Jesus - Luke 6:27 (NLT)

The follower of Jesus has been called to live a *radically different* life to those who are in the world around them. In fact, it's not only different - it's the complete opposite. Jesus doesn't give His followers the option to simply 'tweak' their previous lifestyle, or to merely 'add' His teachings to what they're currently doing. No, those who want to follow Jesus are called to live a *completely different lifestyle* that brings glory to God.

The curtain is drawn back to give us a glimpse of this 'Jesus lifestyle' in Luke 6:27-38. Here, we read how Jesus teaches His followers they need to *love their enemies; to do good to those who hate them; to bless those who want to harm them;* and to *pray for those who have wronged them[1].* This is the complete opposite to the way the world does things. The average person in the world retaliates when somebody offends them, and will often think of ways they can take revenge. They may try to malign their enemy directly to their face, or it may be more subtle - they will bad-mouth or gossip about them to other people in an attempt to destroy their character. Jesus teaches us another way to respond however, which is to *"...love your enemies. Do good to those who hate you. Bless those who call down curses on you. And pray for those who treat you badly"[2].*

Jesus is not sharing a 'good idea' or a philosophy with us - He's giving us an insight into the character of God[3], which is

27

something He Himself demonstrated 'in the flesh' throughout His earthly ministry[4]. This demonstration of God's nature was the fruit of the relationship that Jesus had with His Father. Remarkably, it's what He calls His followers to do also[5], which is to show the world what their Heavenly Father is really like. By *'loving our enemies, doing good to those who hate us, and praying for those who treat us badly"*, we're actually demonstrating the nature of the One who lives in us[6] to those around us. Like Jesus, this can only come about as we grow in our relationship with the Father, and is what brings glory to God[7].

We don't have the ability to do this in our own strength. Thankfully, God has *already* poured His love into our hearts[8], so what was previously impossible for us to do because of our old sin nature, has now become possible. As born-again children of God[9], we have been given His nature by His Spirit[10], which means *we can actually do the things Jesus calls us to do* - empowered by His Spirit who lives in us. It is the presence of <u>His</u> Spirit within us that enables us to live the radical lifestyle that Jesus has called us to. Surrender to God's Holy Spirit within you, so that the grace to love your enemy is given the opportunity to rise up, strengthening you to deal with every situation that comes against you - for His glory.

"Father, thank You for giving me the ability to love those who try to harm me. I choose to deal with every situation I face in the same way You would deal with it, so I surrender today to Your Holy Spirit within me. I allow the grace to forgive, the strength to do good to those who want to hurt me, as well as the commitment to pray for those who persecute me, to rise up from within me so that You are glorified. In Jesus' Name I pray. Amen"

Are You Following Jesus, or Moses?

*"But I warn you — unless your righteousness is better than the
righteousness of the teachers of religious law and the Pharisees,
you will never enter the Kingdom of Heaven!"*
Jesus - Matthew 5:20 (NLT)

When challenged by the blind man whom Jesus had healed, the
Pharisees made it very clear they were disciples of Moses, not
Jesus[1]. What were they saying?

Moses represents the Law that God gave His people at Mount
Sinai[2] - a set of commandments as to how His people should
live. Jesus tells us God is good[3], as well as perfect[4], which is
why the Law given to Moses was *'holy, righteous, and good'*[5]. The
people's continual failure to keep these commandments was
not because there was a problem with the Law - the problem
was with man. *God deliberately gave the Law so that man could see
his problem.* God wanted man to understand that no matter how
hard he tried, he would never be able to come up to His
standard of Holiness (the *'holy, righteous, and good'* Law),
because the sin nature within man prevented it[6]. The Law was
purposely given by God to bring man *'into the knowledge of sin'*[7]
- it was to help man recognise he (or she) has a sin nature that
causes them to fall short of the glory of God[8] (God's required
standards).

By telling man he is condemned if he doesn't keep the _whole_ of
the Law[9], God is bringing man *to the end of himself.* He wants
man to see his own utter hopelessness where righteousness is
concerned, so that he would cease trusting in himself, but

rather look to put his trust in Christ and His righteousness[10]. It is in Christ that God gives man *His own righteousness* as a gift[11], and it's through faith in Christ that man receives it[12]. Faith in Christ brings the individual *from* being under a Law that brought death and condemnation[13], *to* a place where *grace* reigns[14]. The righteousness of God is *already* available for mankind in Christ, but it's only as we turn away from our own righteousness (works of the Law), and put our faith in His righteousness, that we receive it. That's grace!

The Pharisees believed they were right with God because they kept the Law - they trusted their own works in order to be righteous before God. They refused to come to the One who came to fulfil the Law perfectly on their behalf[15], and so rejected God's perfect righteousness that comes to all who put their faith in Jesus[16]. What about you - whose righteousness are you trusting today? Is your relationship with God dependant on your 'works' (the Law), or on the Person Jesus Christ? It's when our faith and trust is *fully*[17] in Jesus and what He's done that God's righteousness is perfected in us, and as we receive from Him, we're then able to walk freely in it for His glory[18].

"Father, thank You for making Your righteousness available to me in Jesus Christ. My right standing with You Lord does not depend on what I've done or haven't done - it's based on what Jesus has done on my behalf. I receive His righteousness by faith, and I choose to walk in it every day so that You are glorified. In Jesus' Name I pray. Amen"

Beware of the Yeast of the Pharisees and Herod

"Jesus warned them, "Watch out! Guard against the yeast
of the Pharisees and of Herod."
Jesus - Mark 8:15 (CEV)

As they crossed the lake, the disciples were discussing the fact they only had one loaf, which wasn't enough to feed everybody. Hearing their conversation, Jesus said to them *"Be careful! Watch out for the yeast of the Pharisees and the yeast of Herod!"*[1]. They thought Jesus was literally talking about them only having one loaf[2], when in fact He was trying to teach them an important *spiritual* lesson[3].

Yeast (or 'leaven') permeates *every part* of the dough when making bread. Jesus wants His followers to understand that the same principle applies *spiritually*, and sends out a warning that we need to be extremely careful regarding which *spiritual yeast* we allow to permeate our hearts. In the account from Mark's Gospel He warns against the *'yeast of the Pharisees and Herod'*[4]; in Matthew's account He also mentions the *'yeast of the Sadducees'*[5]. So what exactly is Jesus warning His followers about?

Jesus was referring to the *teaching* of the Pharisees and Sadducees[6], which as we saw yesterday is a righteousness based on *works*, not on faith in what Jesus has done. These religious leaders were hypocrites[7] because they had an *outward appearance* of holiness[8], yet on the inside their hearts were far from God[9]. They were teaching *the precepts of men*, not the Word of God[10], which meant the life that's in the Word[11] was nullified,

31

not only in their own lives but also in the lives of those they taught[12]. They valued their traditions more highly than what God had said in His Word, twisting it to say what they wanted it to say[13]. Add to this the *'yeast of the Sadducees'*[14] - a group of liberal thinkers who had no issues with questioning the authority of Scripture, and you get a toxic combination which helps us understand why Jesus was constantly rebuking them[15] and warning His followers about their teaching. The *'yeast of Herod'* on the other hand is simply trying to persuade people that a particular political system is the answer to the socio-economic problems the world faces. The truth is however only the Kingdom of God can truly answer society's problems, by changing people's hearts through faith in Jesus Christ .

Jesus talks about another 'yeast' as well - the *'yeast of the Kingdom'*[16]. <u>This is what Jesus wants us to fill our hearts with,</u> because this is the yeast that brings *multiplication and life*. That's why He asked the disciples to recall the feeding of the four and five thousand[17]. It's when we allow *the yeast of the Kingdom* to fully permeate our hearts that faith comes, and with it the miraculous - in this instance thousands being fed with plenty left over. Prayerfully consider today what sort of 'yeast' you are allowing to permeate your heart. Ask God to show you, because it is only the yeast of His Kingdom that will make an eternal difference to you, as well as to your family and the community you live in.

"Father, my prayer today is very simple. Please permeate EVERY PART of my heart with the Yeast of Your Kingdom. My prayer is sincere Lord, and because I ask in faith in Jesus' Name, I thank You Lord for answering. Amen"

Finding a Quiet Place

"Let's go to a place where we can be alone and get some rest."
Jesus - Mark 6:31b (CEV)

It was a busy period for Jesus and His disciples[1], so He suggested they find a quiet place where they could spend some time together and not be disturbed. It didn't work out as they had hoped because the crowds realised where they were going and got there ahead of them[2].

Jesus would share things with His disciples in private that He wasn't prepared to share publicly[3]. He would teach openly through parables, but then wait for the opportunity to talk to His disciples *in private* to make sure they understood what He was teaching[4]. Jesus hasn't changed[5]. In the same way He shared privately with His disciples then, He is keen to share privately with us now, if we're willing to listen[6].

Jesus encourages us to find a *private* space when we're meeting with God - somewhere we won't be disturbed[7]. It's a place where distractions are kept to a minimum so that we can be sensitive to His small, still voice[8]. It's in this private place that God will share His secrets with us[9]. Some of these things have been kept hidden since before Creation, but He is now eager to share them with us[10]. He will reveal to us His _true_ nature of love, goodness and mercy, so that we can approach Him with confidence and boldness[11]. It is in this private place that God will give us wisdom if we're seeking direction from Him[12]. It's here also that the Lord will give us revelation of truth so that we are able to speak on His behalf[13].

As we meditate on God's Word during these quiet times, we'll hear His voice and sense His Life bubbling up within us[14]. We'll also be able to drink in the medicine that is contained within His Word[15] - a medicine that brings healing to our soul, as well as to our bodies[16]. However, we won't be able to fully experience these privileges or the love He has for us unless we first of all make time to find *a place where we can be alone and get some rest* with Him[17].

The greatest honour for any individual is to know God and to hear His voice[18]. We therefore need to seize the opportunity we have been given by making sure we find time in our busy lives to go to a 'place' where we can be alone with God and rest. It's as we take ourselves apart with the Lord that we find rest for our soul and our spiritual 'batteries' are recharged[19]. God has given each one of us the same opportunity to go higher with Him, so let's start looking at the things we're giving our attention to (which may not necessarily be bad), and start making decisions as to whether we need to let go of some of them. This way, we'll have time and space to find *a place where we can be alone and get some rest* with Him[20].

"Father, thank You for inviting me to spend more time with You. My heart is drawn by the prospect Lord, so please would You give me the wisdom, the self-discipline, as well as the thirst I need to make sure I take full advantage of this privilege You are offering me. In Jesus' Name I pray. Amen"

Bearing Fruit as a Disciple of Jesus

"Show that you are my followers by producing much fruit.
This will bring honour to my Father."
Jesus - John 15:8 (ERV)

In today's headline verse, Jesus tells us it's our *fruit* that demonstrates we are His disciples. It's possible as a Christian to say the right things and give the impression we're following Jesus, but if our *fruit* doesn't line up with our confession[1], we need to look carefully at where we are on our journey with the Lord. The fruit that demonstrates we are followers of Jesus is the *fruit of the Spirit* - love, joy, peace, patience, kindness, goodness, faithfulness, gentleness and self-control[2]. This is the fruit that reflects *His* nature and *His* character to the world around us. It's by bearing this type of fruit that we bring glory to God because we're allowing people to see what God is really like[3].

As confessors of Christ, we have a responsibility to be *demonstrators* of Christ as well. Demonstrating fruit such as bitterness, anger, and gossip[4] (as examples) does not bring glory to God - in fact it has the opposite effect because people see us as hypocrites and judgemental which in turn gives them a wrong impression of God. This sort of fruit may have been in our nature before we came to Christ, but now we've received Christ as our Saviour we should be demonstrating the fruit of the Holy Spirit more consistently. We may still see some 'bad fruit' occasionally, particularly early on in our Christian life, but because our old nature has been crucified with Christ[5] and God has given us a new nature[6], it's the fruit of our *new* nature that should now be most evident.

God is not asking us to do anything He has not already given us the power to do - so we're not talking here about something which relies on our own will-power or self-effort. The potential to produce good fruit starts with the truth that we have been *born of the Spirit*[7], and it's out of this *newly created spirit* that the fruit of the Spirit will grow. God wants to create the image of Christ within each one of us[8] (which will produce good fruit), and it's as we *make choices that line up with the Holy Spirit* that we give Him the permission to shape the character of Christ within us[9]. If we're willing to surrender to the leading and guiding of the Holy Spirit through the Word of God, we will undergo a 'metamorphosis'[10] - a transformation that is so radical that the fruit of the Spirit will be produced *naturally* in our lives. This fruit simply becomes the evidence that Christ lives in us and that we are born of the Spirit.

Make the choice today to completely surrender yourself to the transformational work of the Holy Spirit who lives in you[11]. Allow Him to have full reign, so that you bear fruit that brings life to people, not only through your actions but also through the words you speak. As you do this, there is no doubt that God will be glorified[12].

"Lord, I am so thankful for the privilege You have given me. You want to shape the image of Christ within me, and all You're asking me to do Father is to make choices that are consistent with what You say in Your Word. It's by Your power and Your grace that this transformation will occur, not by my effort, so I unreservedly surrender myself to You today and every day, so that You are glorified in and through my life. In Jesus' Name I pray. Amen"

Day 15

Become Servant Hearted

"But don't act like them. If you want to be great, you must be the servant of all the others."
Jesus - Mark 10:43 (CEV)

The apostle John recorded for us how Jesus, on the eve of His crucifixion got up from the table after supper and proceeded to wash the disciples' feet[1]. We can become so familiar with this account that it's possible to miss the significance of it, so let's explore what Jesus wanted His disciples to learn from this act of humility.

God created the heavens and the earth[2] with such precision that not only does He know how many stars He created, He also named them all[3]. He even knows how many hairs each person has on their head[4]. By meditating on God's work of creation, we come to the place of standing in awe of His majesty and splendour[5]. It is sobering to think how this God whose greatness we see in creation, took on flesh in the Person of Jesus Christ and became like one of us - except He was without sin.[6] God Almighty stepped into His own creation[7] so that He could rescue it from the darkness it had been subjected to through the Fall[8]. He did this knowing full well that He would be rejected, and eventually killed by the very ones He had come to rescue[9]. This is remarkable.

It gets even more amazing however, because this God who came to dwell with man[10] *didn't enter His creation to be served,* (even though He had every right to be) - He came to be *the One who would serve*[11]. No words can describe how amazing this is -

that the Almighty One who is worthy to be served by all, came to be the Servant of all - which He demonstrated by washing the disciples' feet. That sort of mind-set is completely alien to mankind, because man is always looking to be served, rather than looking to be the one who serves.

God's Kingdom is *'an upside down kingdom'* - it's completely different to what we are familiar with in the world system. This is what Jesus wanted His disciples to understand, saying to them: *"You know that the rulers in this world lord it over their people, and officials flaunt their authority over those under them. But among you it will be different. Whoever wants to be a leader among you must be your servant."*[12]. He was explaining not only is His Kingdom different, it's actually the _opposite_ to how the world system operates. Therefore, as Kingdom citizens we need to think the way He thinks[13], seeing ourselves as ones who will serve others rather than looking to be served. According to Jesus, this is what greatness looks like in the Kingdom[14].

It's important to seek clarity from God regarding the gifts He has given us[15], as well as take the time to hear the 'where and how' we serve others with those gifts. This is when we'll find our place of fulfilment, but more importantly it's where we're able to demonstrate God's Kingdom to those around us. People won't then have to read John's account to hear about Jesus' servant heart - they will see it in action in you and me. What a privilege!

"Father, I want to learn to serve others in the way that You served. Please release Your servant heart within me Lord and use me to bring You glory. I ask this in the precious Name of Jesus. Amen."

Eliminating Fear

"Do not let your heart be troubled, nor let it be fearful."
Jesus - John 14:27b

On the eve of His crucifixion, Jesus said to His disciples *"I leave my peace with you. I give my peace to you. I do not give it to you as the world does. Do not let your hearts be troubled. And do not be afraid"*[1].

Jesus made it clear that as His disciples, *we have the ability to choose* whether to allow our hearts to be troubled (to be fearful) or not. Telling His disciples *not* to allow their hearts to be troubled would have been an unreasonable demand if it were not possible for them to do it in the first instance. One of the privileges of being a citizen in the Kingdom of God is that the believer has the ability to *choose* not to allow fear to take hold of them. However, this can only come about through an understanding of what Jesus has done through the cross and resurrection, as well as appreciating where He has positioned those who have put their faith in Him.

Through faith in Christ, the believer is delivered <u>*from*</u> the kingdom of darkness where fear reigns, <u>*into*</u> the Kingdom of God where the Prince of Peace reigns[2]. This is a *present tense truth* for those who have placed their faith in Jesus Christ[3]. It means the rule and dominion of fear comes to an end in the life of the person who accepts Jesus as their Lord and Saviour. Fear no longer has authority over them because they are now in a different kingdom. Does this mean they stop feeling fearful from that moment onwards? No it doesn't, because the individual then needs to undergo the process of *renewing their mind* - a moving away from the old 'default' ways of thinking in order to embrace the new, which comes about through spending time with God in His Word. The starting point is to understand that although the *feeling* of fear may be very real, the dominion and authority of the fear has already been broken and so they no longer have to tolerate it in their lives[4].

Fear is from the kingdom of darkness, but Jesus has completely defeated the one who rules that dark kingdom[5]. Jesus is now seated in the place of all authority[6], and through the new spiritual birth God has positioned us with Him[7]. We haven't gone up to heaven to take our position - heaven has come down to us - by His Spirit[8]. It's from this position of being seated *with* Christ that we are able to take our authority over fear and command it to go[9].

The next time fear tries to come upon you, learn to recognise it for what it is - a defeated enemy that you have been given authority over[10]. Take your stand against it with 'the Sword of the Spirit'[11] by speaking God's Word from your mouth. Declare that you refuse to allow your heart to be troubled, and that you consent only to allowing the Prince of Peace to establish His rule in your heart. It's a battle that's worth fighting, because the victory is already ours in Christ Jesus.

"Father, I am so grateful to You for giving me hope. In those dark times when my mind is inundated with thoughts of fear and hopelessness, I now know that this darkness has already been defeated because of what You have done. Give me the courage to stand up against the wickedness that tries to intimidate me, and thank You for giving me Your spiritual Sword to eradicate this enemy from my life. I thank You Lord and bless You in the Name of Jesus. Amen."

(*"Defeating Fear, Panic, and Anxiety - A 30-day Devotional"* gives a more comprehensive teaching on being set free from fear - see Page 85)

Persecution

"And since I, the master of the household, have been called the prince of demons, the members of my household will be called by even worse names!"
Jesus - Matthew 10:25b (NLT)

The follower of Jesus Christ carries an aroma[1]. It's like wearing an expensive perfume, but it's not one that can be picked up by the natural senses because it is *spiritual* in nature. The Christian carries this spiritual fragrance continually, and as they go about their daily lives people will react in different ways to it. This is how the apostle Paul described it: *"Our lives are a Christ-like fragrance rising up to God. But this fragrance is perceived differently by those who are being saved and by those who are perishing. To those who are perishing, we are a dreadful smell of death and doom. But to those who are being saved, we are a life-giving perfume.[2]"* Though this fragrance is beautiful, not everybody appreciates it. In fact, some hate it so much that they will persecute the individual who is carrying it.

Persecution can come from two main directions - the inside, as well as from the outside. The persecution that comes from *within* is when the devil tries to use our 'flesh' (the old sinful nature) to influence our hearts and minds. The old sinful nature does not want to line up with God[3] so the devil will try to use this weakness to get us off course in our journey of following Christ. The persecution that comes from the *outside* is when people deliberately mistreat an individual for being a Christian - this sort of persecution can vary greatly in its nature and intensity. The spectrum of persecution ranges from being rejected or treated differently in work situations, to being tortured, imprisoned, or even killed for having faith in Jesus Christ. Unfortunately we continue to see this in many parts of the world even today. Whatever the source of the persecution, its purpose is always the same - to try to stop the Gospel of Jesus Christ from advancing, both within us[4] (our hearts), as well as to our communities, nations, and the ends of the earth[5].

It is the *fragrance of Christ* that brings the persecution, not the person carrying it. This is because it is a *spiritual* matter, not a natural one. Once we realise the source of persecution is spiritual, we will learn not to take it personally and so won't feel the need to 'fight' the persecutor. It is the spiritual influence behind the person we need to turn our attention to[6], which is why God has given us *spiritual* weapons so we can deal with the persecution we're facing[7]. These weapons are 'divinely powerful'[8] which means they are infused with the power of God Himself. One of the most powerful weapons we can use is love, which is why Jesus tells us to love our enemies and pray for them[9]. Other weapons include the Name of Jesus[10]; the Sword of the Spirit[11] (the Word of God); and prayer[12]. If you are experiencing persecution today, position yourself in God so that He becomes your refuge, fortress, stronghold, and much more[13]. It is in Him we will find our perfect peace to deal with the situations we're facing[14], no matter how overwhelmed we may feel.

"Lord Jesus, help me to accept that persecution of some description is inevitable as I follow You. Please help me to stay strong during those times, drawing on You and the weapons You have given me to deal with the challenges. Help me to love my enemies, so that Your Gospel can advance in the most trying of situations I may face. Thank You Lord for Your constant faithfulness. I pray these things in the Name of Jesus. Amen."

Day 18

Light or Darkness - Our Choice

"Your body gets its light through your eyes. When you have good eyes, all your body has light. But when your eyes are bad, your body is in darkness."
Jesus - Luke 11:34 (WE)

The principle of how a pinhole camera works is very simple. Whatever object the camera is looking at, light from that object enters through the pinhole and forms an image inside the camera. It is the same spiritually. Our eyes are the 'pinhole' that allows light from whatever we're looking at to enter our heart. The Living Bible says it like this: *"Your eyes light up your inward being. A pure eye lets sunshine into your soul. A lustful eye shuts out the light and plunges you into darkness.[1]"*

The image that is formed within us can be light, or it can be darkness - depending on what we're looking at. If we're looking at what God says in His Word, then it is Light we're allowing into our hearts. If the images we're watching on television or on our computer are wholesome, again it's light we're allowing into our hearts. Conversely, when our eyes are looking at darkness - violent or sexual images in films for example, then it will be darkness that enters through the pinhole of our eyes. This is what Jesus means in today's title verse when He refers to our eyes being 'good' or 'bad'. Very simply, what we look at with our eyes determines whether we allow spiritual light, or spiritual darkness into our soul (heart).

It's not just what *we look at* that determines what gets on the inside of us - our *ears* are also a point of entry, as are *the words we speak*. God tells us that if we <u>look,</u> as well as <u>listen</u> to His

Word[2], and then make sure that we _speak_ only those things that He has already declared in His Word[3], then the life and health that is in His Word will become ours[4]. It's no surprise therefore to hear Jesus telling us to allow only light in through our eyes[5]; to be careful what we listen to[6]; and to make sure we watch our words[7].

Being filled with either spiritual light or spiritual darkness as a result of the things we look at, listen to, and say with our mouths _is a spiritual law_. This simply means it is non-negotiable and works the same for everybody. Nobody can watch a violent and dark film, or listen to sexually explicit lyrics and not be affected negatively by the experience (spiritually), any more than they could step off a high building and not be affected by the law of gravity (physically). This is because it is a _law_ and it will be enforced whether we are aware of it or not, or whether we choose to believe it or not. The only influence we have in the matter is _the ability to choose what we allow to put before our eyes and in our ears in the first instance_. Once the choice is made however, there is nothing further we can do regarding the outcome because the spiritual law comes into operation. Let's make sure therefore that by God's grace we consistently choose those things that bring light, so that we allow the spiritual law to work in our favour, not to our detriment.

"Father, thank You for helping me understand how important it is for me to be careful with what I allow into my heart through my eyes, my ears, and my mouth. I want to take this issue seriously Lord because I want to be full of light - Your Light. Therefore I ask You Father to give me the grace I need to make any changes, so that Your light would fill my heart and that I would become a beacon to others who are in darkness. In Jesus' Name I ask this. Amen."

Day 19

Don't Be Distracted

*"Anyone who lets himself be distracted from the work I plan for him
is not fit for the Kingdom of God."*
Jesus - Luke 9:62 (TLB)

One of Jesus' followers[1] asked Him if he could go home to say
goodbye to his family before travelling with Him[2]. Jesus' reply
was *"...whoever starts to plow and looks back is not fit for God's
kingdom.[3]"* On the surface that may sound quite harsh, so let's
try to understand what Jesus was really saying.

I don't believe Jesus had a problem with the man going back to
say his goodbyes, any more than Elijah (a 'type' of Jesus) had a
problem with Elisha going back to say goodbye to his family[4].
Jesus was simply drawing this man's attention to the danger of
being *distracted from his calling* as he went back to say goodbye.
On returning to a setting he had been comfortable and familiar
with, Jesus wanted him to be aware that his heart could be
drawn back into that environment. This would then result in
the call of God on his life being negated. I think Jesus was
saying something like *"be careful that what you've left behind in
order to follow Me doesn't draw you back and cause you to lose focus
on what I've called you into"*.

The temptation to look back and start reminiscing on what
we've left behind to follow Jesus is a real one. It is also
dangerous, because it can prevent us from moving forward into
the fullness of what God has called us in to. This is what
happened to the Israelites in the wilderness. When things
started to get challenging for them they started to moan and

complain to Moses about the things they missed from their time in Egypt[5]. They had forgotten about the slavery and suffering they had endured, and also that God had rescued them *from* that situation in order to give them a better future[6]. It didn't end well for those Israelites who constantly looked back at what they'd left behind because they died in the wilderness even though the Promised Land was theirs for the taking. It was only the generation who had been born in the wilderness, those who had no experience of Egypt that eventually went in to possess the land of Canaan[7].

Where is your focus today? Is it firmly on the call God has placed on your life, or are you allowing those things from your past to pull you back? Even the apostle Paul had to grapple with this, saying: *"My brothers, I do not yet think that I have got all the things of Christ. But there is one thing that I am doing. I forget what is behind me and reach out to what is ahead of me.[8]"* Despite the severe hardships he was enduring[9], Paul didn't look back at the life of relative luxury he once had because the revelation of how amazing Jesus is had opened up before him. He had glimpsed the magnificence of Jesus, causing him to remain focused on the calling God had placed on his life[10]. Let's make sure this is true of us as well; that we leave behind those things which are trying to draw us back from God's calling on our lives[11] by keeping our eyes firmly fixed on how lovely Jesus is[12]. It's as we keep our eyes on Jesus that we see the fruit of what He's called us into[13].

"Father, it is so easy to look back and be tempted to take my eyes off You. Please help me to focus on Your beauty, and the calling You have placed on my life, because that is where I know I will find true fulfilment. I thank You Lord for calling me, and I choose to remain focused on You, and the Kingdom work You have called me into. In Jesus' Name I pray. Amen."

Day 20

Taking Communion By Faith

"Do this to remember me."

Jesus - Luke 22:19b (GW)

The elements of communion are very simple - bread and wine. These simple elements give no indication whatsoever of the lavish banquet that God is offering to those who accept His invitation to participate. It's only as the curtain is drawn back that we begin to see how much of an extravagant feast God has prepared for those who partake of His Son[1].

The elements of communion represent more than what *happened* to Jesus on the Cross - they also represent what Jesus *achieved* at the Cross. Taking communion is not simply about remembering the historical event on Calvary two thousand years ago. It is also the means by which we remember what the *outcome* of that event was, and are then able to apply this truth to our own lives through faith. On the Cross, Jesus took upon Himself the sin that once held us in bondage[2] so that we could be set free from its slavery[3]. Communion is a time to remember, as well as to celebrate the reality of that truth in our lives.

Jesus also took the curse of sickness and disease upon Himself on the Cross[4]. Again, communion is a time to remember the chastisement He underwent, so that *by faith* we can receive the healing and wholeness He won for us[5]. This is only part of God's banquet however, because at communion we also give thanks and celebrate the love, grace, forgiveness, mercy, security, protection, peace, joy (the list goes on) that God has provided for all who place their faith in Jesus Christ.

Approaching communion in a ritualistic way means our eyes will remain closed to the depth of God's goodness which is held within the sacrament. Communion has been given *for our sake,* so that as we take of the elements we can remember the *covenant* God has brought us into because of our faith in Jesus Christ[6]. Though simple, communion is profound. Though the elements are ordinary, they are a spiritual feast to those who understand what they represent. I pray that the eyes of our hearts are further opened to the depth of God's goodness, which He has poured out on every individual who receives His Son by faith[7]. God is inviting us to partake of His great grace through the simplest of elements - let's make sure we first of all remember, and then by faith receive everything He has won for us.

"Lord, thank You for giving me the sacrament of communion. I ask Lord that You continue to open the eyes of my heart so that I can see the riches this simple act holds. I ask You to take me deeper into the reality of what You have done for me on the Cross, which is the reflection of Your goodness towards me. I ask this in the Name of Jesus. Amen."

Day 21

Be Prepared For His Return

"Therefore, be alert, because you don't know on what day
your Lord will return."
Jesus - Matthew 24:42 (GW)

Jesus taught that He *is* coming back, but that no one knows exactly when it will be[1]. He emphasised to His followers the need to be ready for that day[2]. Today's devotional centres on Matthew chapters twenty-four and twenty-five, so it would be helpful to read these two chapters before moving on.

Jesus starts by teaching about the signs which will occur in the lead up to His return[3]. Mark and Luke also record these events[4]. He then goes on to share a short parable about the fig tree, explaining that in the same way leaves growing on a fig tree indicate a new season is approaching, the signs Jesus talks about also indicate that His return is drawing near[5].

Jesus then shares a series of parables explaining what the attitude of His followers should be as they wait for His return. The first parable talks about a servant being put in charge of his master's household[6]. Here Jesus is revealing how believers need to make sure they take their responsibilities as Christians seriously. Every Christian has been given a degree of responsibility and trust - family, neighbourhood, work, and church leadership are examples. How we manage the areas of responsibility we have been given is a sobering matter, with Jesus warning us about the danger of taking our responsibilities lightly[7].

49

The parable of the ten virgins waiting for the bridegroom to attend a wedding feast[8] is Jesus' way of explaining how the believer needs to make sure they are continually filled with the Holy Spirit[9]. This comes by first of all asking to be filled[10], then continuing to spend time in prayer, worship, reading God's Word, and walking in obedience to Him.

The final parable is about a master entrusting his possessions to his servants when he goes on a journey[11]. This parable speaks about how God *expects every believer to do something with the gifts He has given them.* It's as we use our gifts for good (multiplication) that we are given more responsibility. We need to make sure we're not like the servant who had an incorrect perception of God, being frightened of using what he'd been given[12].

Chapter twenty-five ends with the judgement that will happen on Christ's return[13]. Jesus wants His followers to be ready so they can be counted with the righteous who are ushered into eternal life[14]. Christ's righteousness in us, received as a gift[15], will cause us to have oil in our lamps, which in turn enables us to show the compassion and mercy Jesus will be looking for when He returns[16]. Take some time today to consider how you are managing the areas of responsibility God has given you; what measures you have in place to make sure the Holy Spirit knows He is welcome in your heart; as well as checking that you are using the gifts you have been given in a way that glorifies Him.

"Lord Jesus, thank You for reminding me that You will be coming back some day. My prayer is simple Lord - please help me to diligently manage the gifts and responsibilities You have entrusted to me so that I am ready when You return. I ask this in Your Name Lord. Amen."

You Are The Light Of The World

"You are the light of the world. A city set on a hill cannot be hidden."
Jesus - Matthew 5:14

It all starts with Jesus. He is the Light of the world[1]. As we make a decision to follow Him we begin to walk in His Light, and then through the born-again experience we become 'sons of Light' (irrespective of gender)[2]. Even though Jesus has ascended to Heaven, the world still has the Light because He now lives in every believer[3]. By saying to His followers *'You are the light of the world'*[4], Jesus is effectively handing over the baton of being the light of the world to you and me.

If there were no Christians on the earth (in the world), there would be no light. I'm not referring to the physical light that comes from the sun, but the *spiritual* light that brings hope. It is this spiritual Light living within each Christian that is preventing the world from being overwhelmed by spiritual darkness, because where there is no light, all that's left is darkness. Christians are not here to simply 'hold the fort', waiting for the cavalry to come to the rescue (Jesus' return) - we're here to make a difference now - because the nature of light is that it dispels darkness. Every Christian is here to take back territory from the kingdom of darkness, so that the government of Jesus can rule in every corner of the earth[5].

The individual who is carrying the Light of Christ is here to plunder the kingdom of darkness so that the Kingdom of God can be ushered in. We're here to release captives from the bondage of addiction and hopelessness; to bring healing to people whose lives satan is destroying through sickness and disease[6]; and to declare mercy and forgiveness to those who are held in the darkness of guilt, shame, and depression[7]. We're here to give Life - the very Life of Jesus because He lives in us[8]. No matter what bondage the kingdom of darkness may be subjecting a person to, it's no match for the Kingdom of God. It is *impossible* for the gates of hell to keep an individual bound when we, as carriers of the Light come knocking on the door of their hearts and offer them the good news of the Kingdom[9].

As a carrier of the Light, every Christian has a responsibility to play their part in advancing God's Kingdom. This is a big responsibility, but it's not burdensome because with the assignment comes the joy and the grace to fulfil the mission[10]. We may struggle with the concept that we can make a difference to those around us. We're right - *we* can't make a difference - but the One whom we carry can. It is the One who is Light, living in us, who makes the difference - our responsibility is to make sure we allow Him to shine through us. The assignment doesn't allow us to hide ourselves from the world[11], but rather to share the Light in such a way that brings glory to God[12]. As we choose to be obedient to His voice, the Light we are carrying can, and will make a difference to someone's life - even today.

"Father, thank You that I am carrying You - the Light who is the hope of the world. My desire Lord is to shine Your light on those whom You bring across my path. I make myself available to You today, and every day so that Your Light within me is obvious to those whom I come into contact with. In Jesus' Name I pray this. Amen."

Day 23

Messengers With A Message

"As you go, tell people that the kingdom of heaven is here."
Jesus - Matthew 10:7 (WE)

Jesus preached the good news that the Kingdom of God is near, and that it's available to all who put their faith in Him[1]. The Kingdom of God is no longer limited to Heaven - it has come down to earth in the Person of Jesus Christ, and through faith in Him everybody gets an invitation to enter[2]. This is the essence of His message, and that's the good news He has tasked His followers to share with others[3].

Jesus has dealt with the hindrance that prevented man from entering His Kingdom (sin)[4]; allowing the individual who has faith in Christ to enter into God's presence boldly[5]. As an act of His grace, God has clothed each person whose faith is in Christ with the righteous robes needed to sit at His banqueting table[6]. Everything has already been taken care of[7] - our part is to simply *receive* the goodness of God as presented to us in Jesus Christ[8]. The invitation is stamped 'Grace', not 'Works', which is why it's such good news!

It is in the Kingdom of God we find the mercy we need to have our sin forgiven[9]. It's when we're in His Kingdom that we find ourselves delivered from spiritual bondages and addictions. It's in this Kingdom we find the healing we need for our bodies, minds, and emotions[10], as well as the hope, peace, and future we've been created to enjoy[11]. This is the Kingdom that Jesus not only brought, but also *demonstrated* through His ministry.

53

The miracles of multiplication, the healing of sick bodies, and the deliverance of those who were demon possessed were a *demonstration* of the truth and reality that the Kingdom of God had come to earth.

Jesus' ministry didn't just demonstrate that God's Kingdom had come; it was also the evidence of how God's Kingdom is *superior* to the kingdom of darkness. The kingdom that held people in sickness, bondage, and hopelessness was *driven out* by the power of God[12], in order that the Kingdom which brings health, freedom, and deliverance could be ushered in[13].

Jesus tells us *"as we go, we need to tell people the kingdom of God is here"*[14]. It's as we go about our daily lives that God will give us opportunities to tell people that Jesus heals, and that He brings freedom as well as hope. We don't need to carry a soapbox - we can share the good news over a cup of tea as long as we've got someone who wants to listen. Sharing with people the hope that we have is a privilege[15], and it's as we pray with individuals that we invite the Kingdom to come into their lives[16]. The Kingdom of God is great news - let's make sure we don't keep it to ourselves.

"Father, thank You for opening my eyes to the good news of Your Kingdom. As I go about my daily life Lord, I ask that You give me opportunities to share with others what You have shared with me. When those opportunities present themselves, I ask for the grace and wisdom I need to make sure they hear You, not me. Thank You for the privilege of sharing You Lord. In Jesus' Name I pray. Amen."

Day 24

Restored By Grace

"'Simon son of John, do you love me?' 'Yes, Lord,' Peter said,
'You know I love you.' 'Then take care of my sheep'"

Jesus to Simon Peter - John 21:16 (NLT)

The apostle Peter was remarkable. To start with, he left a thriving business[1] to follow Jesus[2]. Then we have Peter being the only disciple to step out of the boat in the middle of the storm even though the others had the same opportunity[3]. Jesus trusted Peter, together with John and James to come with Him into Jairus' house - everyone else except Jairus and his wife had been told to leave while Jesus healed the little girl[4]. Peter was also someone Jesus took up the mountain to witness His transfiguration, and he became so excited he wanted to build shelters so they could stay there[5]. Peter's account doesn't just include 'mountain-top' experiences however - he also had some desperately low times as well.

Following Jesus' arrest, Peter was in the courtyard of the building where the Sanhedrin would meet the next morning to put Jesus on trial[6]. A servant-girl challenged him as being one of Jesus' followers, but he denied it outright[7]. The same thing happened a second time, and again Peter denied having any association with Jesus[8]. When it happened a third time, Peter swore and cursed as he denied his Master, trying to sound more convincing[9]. The man who had left everything for Jesus, who had walked on water and had witnessed Jesus performing countless miracles, was now denying the One he loved. Only hours earlier he had pledged his allegiance to the death for

Jesus[10], but realising what he'd done in denying Him he started to weep uncontrollably[11].

Like me, your heart goes out to Peter. But if we fast-forward a few weeks we'll see that his story is one of victory, not failure. Now back in Jerusalem, Peter is preaching openly about Jesus and thousands are being saved[12]. A lame man gets healed because of his ministry[13] and people are bringing their sick out onto the streets so that they can be healed by Peter's shadow[14]. This is a long way from his dramatic failure a few weeks earlier, so what had happened to Peter? Firstly, Peter knew Jesus was alive - he'd seen him for himself[15]. Secondly, Peter had been restored by Jesus, because Jesus knew Peter's heart was for Him, not against Him[16]. Then thirdly, Peter was baptised in the Holy Spirit, and then continued in that place of being full of the Spirit[17].

There's a lesson here for each one of us no matter how small or large our failures are. In the middle of his bitter weeping, Peter could never have imagined what his future in Jesus would look like - even in such a short time. When we're in that place of disappointment because of our failures in letting Jesus down, let's remember Peter's story. There is a tomorrow, and as we can see from Peter our tomorrow with Jesus is far better and bigger than we could ever imagine. Let's not allow our failures to define our identity, but be determined to allow the mercy, goodness, and redemptive power of Christ to restore us and then lead us to the place where He wants us to go[18].

"Lord Jesus, I am truly sorry for every single time I've let You down - either through an outright denial of You, or because I've not stood up for You when I know I should have. Please forgive me Lord. Thank You that I have a tomorrow, and it's because of Your grace, in the power of the Holy Spirit that I now go forward into all You have planned for me. I thank You in Jesus' Name. Amen."

Day 25

Walking In Divine Authority

"These are the miraculous signs that will accompany believers:
They will use the power and authority of my name to force demons out of
people.... They will place their hands on the sick and cure them."
Jesus - Mark 16:17a - 18b (GW)

Every disciple of Jesus Christ is given the authority to use His Name. It is not given to an elite few, but to *every person* who is born-again and baptised in the Holy Spirit[1]. Divine authority is not the result of who or what we are - the authority is there because of the One who lives inside us[2].

It is when we understand what it means to be a spokesperson for someone that we will understand what it means to speak in the Name of Jesus. Speaking in the Name of Jesus means we're speaking from a position of having all the attributes that His Name possesses. It means we speak from a place of spiritual victory, because Jesus has already won the war[3]. It means we speak from a place of power and authority, because all power and authority have been given to Jesus. It is in the authority He has been given that Jesus sends out His disciples to preach the good news of the Kingdom[4]. He is not sending us out in our *own* authority, nor in our *own* name, because that doesn't carry any weight. He is sending us out in *His* authority, and in *His* Name, because that's where the power and authority lies.

Jesus has given us His authority so the Kingdom of God can be expanded - which brings glory to God[5]. When people are released from bondage and brought into freedom through the Name of Jesus, God is glorified[6]. When we lay hands on sick people in the Name of Jesus and they recover, God is glorified[7]. In bringing freedom to those who are in bondage, and health to those who are sick, the follower of Jesus Christ is expanding the government rule of God, which is the assignment Jesus has given His disciples[8]. The kingdom that brought sickness, disease, and bondage[9] is expelled, in order that the kingdom that brings freedom, health, and peace can be brought in[10].

Seeing ourselves as 'ordinary' Christians is good in one way because it shows humility and so all the glory goes to God[11]. But remaining in the place of regarding ourselves as ordinary is dangerous because it holds us back from the truth that in Christ we are *extraordinary*[12]. How can a person who has been born-again of the Holy Spirit[13], who has the Creator of the universe living inside them[14] be anything less than extraordinary! From the place of humility, we need to understand who we are in Christ and then live our lives out of that truth so that we begin to experience its reality. Let's make sure we take the authority we have been given seriously. Even though they don't realise it, the people in the world are waiting for those who know who they are in Christ to bring God's Kingdom to them, so they can experience its transformational power![15]

"Father, thank You for giving me the authority that's in Your Name. Help me to grow in the knowledge of who I am in You, and what You have called me to do in Your Name so that You are glorified. I thank You Lord in Jesus' Name. Amen."

The Call To Make Disciples

Day 26

Disciples Will Become Like Their Teacher

"A disciple is not above his teacher, nor a slave above his master. It is enough for the disciple that he become like his teacher, and the slave like his master."
Jesus - Matthew 10:24-25a

In today's headline verse, Jesus teaches how the disciple will *'become like his teacher'*. He's effectively saying that as we follow Him, we will become like Him. Discipleship is the journey by which this change takes place, because it is through discipleship that the image of Christ is formed within the follower[1]. As the nature of Christ begins to form on the inside, the disciple is able to reveal to the world what God is really like.

Forming the nature of Christ on the inside of a person means that discipleship is a *heart* issue, not a *head* one. Becoming Christ-like is not the result of learning more information - it is the result of allowing the Holy Spirit to bring change at a heart level. It's as we surrender daily to the Holy Spirit, spending time with Him in prayer and the Word that we give Him permission to form the image of Christ inside us. A continual obedience to the voice of the Spirit will take us to the place where we become more and more *'like our Teacher'*[2].

When Jesus walked on the earth people were amazed at His wisdom[3]. But it wasn't just His wisdom that people were attracted to - they were attracted to *His nature* as well. Jesus' *compassion* drew people because it gave them hope[4]. His *gentleness* and *mercy* meant people felt safe to approach Him, believing they would find forgiveness[5]. These qualities came

61

out of His *heart,* not His head[6]. Jesus didn't simply come to give the world *information* about God - He *embodied* the Living God so that people could also experience the *nature* of God[7]. This is what we're called to do as well, but a discipleship based on head knowledge alone can't do this because it doesn't develop the nature of Christ within the heart. Biblical knowledge is important, but true discipleship has to go beyond simply giving information (theology) - it needs to impact the heart of the person who is following Christ, as well as their minds. That's why the role of the Holy Spirit in discipleship is critical. He is the only One who can form the image of Christ on the inside, enabling the person to accurately reveal God to the world.

Our responsibility with discipleship is to surrender to the work of the Holy Spirit so He can form the character of Christ in our hearts. There's no point in us trying to 'work' at being like Jesus - the change needs to happen at a heart level first, through the work of the Holy Spirit, then out of that change will come the fruit[8]. We need to give the Holy Spirit lordship over everything - our heart, will, and emotions, as well as our words, actions, and possessions. Surrendering *everything* to Him is not a duty - it's a privilege. Why would we want to hold on to the things that bring death[9], when God is offering us life - life in all its fullness?[10.]

"Father, thank You that You are working in my life. Thank You that You have a plan for me, and that Your plan is built on having the image of Christ formed within me. I surrender to You Lord and give You full freedom to change me so that it is You, and You alone that is reflected through me. In Jesus' Name I pray. Amen."

Jesus Wants His Disciples To Reproduce His Ministry

"I can guarantee this truth:
Those who believe in me will do the things that I am doing."
Jesus - John 14:12a (GW)

Jesus was serious when He said to His disciples *'those who believe in me will do the things that I am doing'*[1]. He wasn't dangling a carrot before them that was impossible to reach, nor was He giving them false expectations. Jesus was presenting His followers with a truth - that those who believe in Him *will* do the things He did. Let's explore what Jesus did so that we know what to expect as we minister in His Name.

Jesus was anointed with the Holy Spirit so that He could *'tell the Good News to the poor'*[2]. The Good News Jesus shared wasn't limited to the forgiveness of sin[3] - it also included freedom from spiritual oppression, healing for those who were sick, as well as the favour of God now being available because Jesus had brought the Kingdom[4]. The miracles Jesus performed were the demonstration that the Kingdom of God had come[5] - He then sent His disciples out to do the same[6]. Jesus hasn't changed[7], which means He is still sending out disciples to proclaim the good news of the Kingdom today. It is *us* He is sending now - all those who have put their faith in Him. He's sending *us* to bring deliverance to the captives, to lay hands on the sick so they recover, and to preach forgiveness of sin - all because of what He has done through the Cross and resurrection[8].

The prospect of being sent out to reproduce Jesus' ministry can be daunting, until we realise we've been given the same enabling power that Jesus had[9]. Even though Jesus was declared God at His birth[10], He didn't perform any miracles until He'd been baptised in the Holy Spirit. How much more then do we need the Holy Spirit! It was the *empowering of the Holy Spirit* that enabled Jesus to demonstrate the Kingdom of God, and it is the same for us. In sending Jesus to proclaim the Kingdom, God gave Jesus the Spirit *'without measure'*[11]. In sending out His disciples, Jesus does the same because He says *'as the Father has sent Me, I also send you'*[12]. There's no expectation for us to reproduce Jesus' ministry in our own strength. We're meant to acknowledge our complete weakness and then look to the promise of the Father[13], which comes to us through being given the Holy Spirit *'without measure'*.

Not everybody is called to preach the Gospel to an audience of millions. But every one of us can share the Good News over a cup of tea with someone who asks us about the hope we have[14]. Not everybody is called to lead a miracle crusade, but all of us are called to lay hands on the sick so they are healed. Each and every follower is equipped by the Holy Spirit to command addictions and bondages to leave in Jesus' Name so that people are set free. The setting will be different for everyone, and our approach will be in accordance with our personality, but the results will be consistent because it is the Holy Spirit who brings the fruit[15]. Jesus is not only calling *other* people to do the things He did - He's also calling *you and me!*

"Lord, thank You for calling me to take Your Good News to the world that is around me. I choose not to allow my weaknesses to be a barrier, but surrender myself completely to the strength that is available to me in the Holy Spirit. In Jesus' Name I pray. Amen."

Day 28

Jesus Needs Help

"A large crop is in the fields, but there are only a few workers"
Jesus - Matthew 9:37 (CEV)

Matthew records for us a particularly busy period in Jesus' ministry. Over two chapters (Matthew 8 & 9) he tells us how Jesus heals a leper[1]; heals the Centurion's servant[2]; heals Peter's mother-in-law[3]; as well as healing <u>crowds</u> of people[4]. He delivers two men possessed with demons[5]; heals a paralysed man who was lowered through the roof[6]; and also a woman who pushed through the crowd so she could touch the edge of His garment[7]. He delivers a demon-possessed man who was mute[8], as well as the young daughter of the local synagogue official[9]. It was a heavy workload - *'going through all the cities and villages'* to share the Gospel, as well as teaching in synagogues on the Sabbath. He healed *'<u>every</u> sickness and disease'* that presented itself to Him[10].

It's at the end of recording these events that Matthew shares with us something Jesus said to His disciples - *"...the harvest is huge. But there are only a few workers. So ask the Lord of the harvest to send workers out into his harvest field."*[11] Even though He'd already achieved a huge amount, Jesus was trying to get the disciples to understand He couldn't do everything by Himself - He needed the Lord who owns this harvest to send others to help. The next thing that happens in the narrative is that Jesus sends out His disciples, giving *them* His power and authority to cast out demons and to heal every kind of sickness and disease[12]. He's already started to answer the prayer He Himself initiated.

Jesus tells His disciples to "*...wake up and look around. The fields are already ripe for harvest.*"[13] The harvest Jesus is referring to is people, with Matthew telling us that compassion rose up within Him as He saw how distressed and helpless they were[14]. Jesus is saying exactly the same thing to His followers today - *'wake up and look around. The fields are already ripe for harvest.'*[13] If we take the time to look around us, we'll understand what Jesus means. What we see is suffering, hopelessness, and despair. We see people struggling with sickness, addiction, and depression. We don't need to look far to see people who are insecure, fearful, and desperate. Jesus has compassion for them just like He did when the scene from Matthew 9:36 presented itself before Him, but today it's *us* He's asking to go out to reap the harvest.

Many of us have personal experience of some of these situations and know how Jesus has brought us out. Now it's our turn - we need to *'freely give just as we were freely given'*[15]. We don't have any excuses because Jesus doesn't expect us to meet the need out of our own resources. He is more than willing to give us *His* power and authority in the same way He gave it to the first disciples[16]. Jesus is saying to us today, *"Will you help Me bring healing to these people? Will you allow My compassion and grace to rise up within you? Will you go in My Name and bring spiritual freedom to those who are distressed and hopeless?"* We are the only ones who can answer these questions for ourselves; but Jesus is waiting for an answer.

"Lord, thank You for what You have done, and continue to do in my life. I give myself to You Lord to help reap the harvest You desire. I present myself wholly to You, and declare that I am willing to go in the power, strength, and grace that You give me. In Jesus' Name I pray. Amen."

Day 29

Making Discipleship A Priority

"So you must go and make disciples of all nations. Baptize them in the name of the Father and of the Son and of the Holy Spirit."
Jesus - Matthew 28:19 (NIrV)

If Jesus had a list of priorities He wanted to accomplish during His earthly ministry, making disciples was definitely one of them. Even before He started performing miracles[1] Jesus was calling people to follow Him[2]. As we continue in the Gospels we read how Jesus spent a large amount of His time teaching and equipping His disciples privately. His earthly ministry was only three years long, yet rather than spending all His time healing and delivering more and more people, Jesus chose to spend a significant part of it teaching and equipping His disciples. These two factors alone give us an indication of the tremendous value Jesus placed on discipleship.

Jesus came to change history, but without the disciples, history would not have been changed. Without the disciples, the message of salvation in Jesus Christ would not have gone any further - it would have ended with Jesus. This is a sobering thought, yet it's the reality of how vital discipleship is to the message of the Gospel, which is why Jesus invested so heavily in it. He wanted to ensure that the salvation He was on the verge of securing for mankind would be proclaimed and made available to all nations after His Ascension[3].

Jesus' model of discipleship meant His disciples were not only able to take the *message* of salvation to the world - they could also *demonstrate* its authenticity through 'signs and wonders'[4].

Jesus taught them to do the exact same things He had done[5] - which included healing the sick and casting out demons[6]. His investment of time and effort meant Jesus was no longer limited to what only He could do. He was multiplying Himself so that His Kingdom could reach more and more people[7].

Jesus discipled His followers in such a way they carried on where He left off. His 'model' was obviously successful because their ministry is recorded in the Book of Acts[8]. If we are going to be obedient to Jesus' call to *make disciples of all nations'[9]*, we have a responsibility to look at how Jesus taught His followers, and then learn from His model. Jesus *taught* His disciples; He *demonstrated* to them how to minister the Kingdom of God in power and authority; and He also *gave them opportunities* so they could have 'hands on' experience of ministering healing and deliverance. There is one additional factor however that forms the foundation of Jesus' discipleship 'programme' - *relationship*. The disciples had a relationship with Jesus, and He with them. The practical elements we see in Jesus' model are essential inclusions in any programme that's hoping to be true to Jesus' call to take the Gospel to the world, but everything has to be founded on a relationship with Him.

We have to give making disciples the same high priority that Jesus gave it. To do this we need to look seriously at *the way* He discipled those who followed Him, so that the Gospel of His Kingdom will continue to be proclaimed as He intended - in both word and deed[10].

"Lord Jesus, I recognise the great value of discipleship. I ask You to enable me to be an excellent disciple, both in my own personal journey with You, as well as when You bring me to the place where You're asking me to disciple others. In Your Name Jesus I ask these things. Amen."

Copying Jesus' Discipleship Model

"Teach them to obey __everything__ I have commanded you."

Jesus - Matthew 28:20a (NIrV - emphasis mine)

We read in the Book of Acts how the miraculous ministry of Jesus continued even though He had returned to the Father. This was because Jesus had discipled others to continue His ministry. We can therefore conclude that Jesus' *method* of discipling was extremely successful. Jesus knew that His way of discipling would bring success, which is why in commissioning His first disciples to go and make more disciples, He instructed them to teach the next generation (of disciples) __everything__ He had taught them[1]. He didn't give them any freedom to change what He Himself had taught them, because He knew that as long as they duplicated what He had done, the potential to make disciples who were equipped to replicate His ministry would continue ad infinitum.

The Church has a responsibility to copy Jesus' discipleship methods because we've not been given permission to create our own. It's when Jesus' model of discipleship is changed or diluted that we find ourselves in the situation where we don't see the results Jesus had with His first disciples. It's foolishness to expect to see the same results, if we're not employing the same methods. In acknowledging His success, it makes perfect sense to look at how Jesus discipled the first twelve and then learn from Him.

We touched yesterday on the four fundamental elements Jesus incorporated into His discipleship model - *TEACHING about the*

69

Kingdom of God; DEMONSTRATING how to heal the sick and bring deliverance to the oppressed; GIVING OPPORTUNITIES for them to do the same; all built on a *RELATIONSHIP with Him.* Though Jesus hasn't left us a formula, we can see from the Gospels how these elements provide a template for us to work from. The likelihood is that we'll fall short of *perfectly* reproducing the model He demonstrated so wonderfully. But at least if we try, we'll be that much closer to getting the same results Jesus had, rather than ignoring His model and trying to create our own.

Heaven's mandate to the Church is to make disciples so that Jesus' ministry to the world can continue. He wants His Kingdom rule to spread. The closer we can adhere to how Jesus made disciples, the more successful we will be at fulfilling this commission because more and more disciples will be equipped to do what Jesus did[2]. Discipleship is absolutely essential in seeing God's Kingdom grow - both at a personal level (in our own hearts); as well as in the world around us. Discipleship is *God's chosen method* of seeing His Kingdom expand, so if it's important to Him, it has to be important to us. It's through discipleship that we ourselves experience the abundant life of Jesus[3], and it's also through discipleship that the government rule of the Prince of Peace spreads across the whole of the world[4]. Please pray with me that the Lord of the harvest will send out more workers into His harvest - even today[5].

"Lord, thank You for speaking to me about discipleship over these past few weeks. I continue to surrender myself fully to following You as a disciple. As I grow in You, please use me to disciple others, remembering that You have already gone before me to show me how. I give myself to You for Your glory; for the building up of Your Church; and for the extending of Your Kingdom here on earth. In Jesus' Name I pray this. Amen."

Endnotes

(Scriptural references)

Endnotes

Day 1

1. Matthew 4:19 (NLT)
2. Matthew 4:18-20
3. Matthew 4:21-22
4. John 1:43
5. Matthew 9:9; Mark 2:14; Luke 5:27-28
6. Matthew 13:44-46; John 6:68-69
7. Mark 10:17-22
8. John 6:59-66
9. John 3:15; 6:63

Day 2

1. Proverbs 8:1-11; 9:1-6; John 5:39
2. John 3:34; 8:26; 14:10; 17:8
3. Luke 24:27, 44-45; John 5:39, 46
4. John 6:63
5. Matthew 11:29
6. Proverbs 8:4-7; 9:4-6; Isaiah 55:1-3; 1 Corinthians 1:26-29
7. John 6:68
8. Matthew 7:24-27
9. Luke 6:40
10. 1 Corinthians 8:1
11. Isaiah 29:13; Matthew 15:8-9; Mark 7:6-7; Romans 12:1-2
12. Matthew 13:11-12; Mark 4:24-25; Luke 19:26
13. Romans 8:29; 2 Corinthians 3:18; Colossians 3:10
14. 2 Corinthians 5:20
15. John 14:12; Romans 8:19; 1 John 2:6

Day 3

1. 1 Cor 3:1-4
2. 1 John 2:6
3. Romans 8:29; 2 Corinthians 3:18; Colossians 3:10
4. John 14:12; 1 John 2:6
5. Romans 8:5; Galatians 5:16
6. Galatians 5:19-21
7. Luke 15:7, 10

Day 4

1. Mark 10:22-23; John 6:66-67
2. Matthew 6:24; Mark 10:23; Luke 12:15
3. Matthew 13:22; Mark 4:19
4. Luke 16:11 (NLT)
5. Matthew 6:33 (NLT)
6. Matthew 6:31-33
7. Matthew 6:32
8. Ephesians 3:20; Philippians 4:19

Day 5

1. Matthew 10:39
2. Psalm 139:16; Jeremiah 29:11-13; Matthew 16:25; Mark 8:35
3. John 10:3-4, 11
4. Romans 8:29; 2 Corinthians 3:18; Colossians 3:10
5. Matthew 10:39; 16:25; Mark 8:35; Luke 9:24
6. John 10:10

Day 6

1. Matthew 4:19 NLT
2. John 14:12; 14:28; 16:5, 16:10; 16:16-17, 28
3. *In John 16:16 the Greek word for 'short time' is 'mikrón'. A fuller definition of this Greek word can be seen in Strong's Concordance (G3397).*
4. John 16:7
5. John 14:18-21
6. John 14:23-28
7. John 14:17
8. John 20:19-22; Acts 2:1-4
9. Acts 8:29; 10:19-21; 11:12; 13:4; 16:6-7
10. Jeremiah 31:34
11. John 14:21
12. John 10:2-5
13. Psalm 103:20
14. John 17:17
15. John 16:13
16. John 16:14-15
17. John 14:6
18. Jeremiah 29:11

Endnotes

Day 7

1. Luke 24:13-16
2. Luke 24:27
3. Luke 24:44-47
4. John 5:39-40
5. John 5:46 (NLT) - emphasis mine
6. Matthew 5:17
7. Matthew 13:52 (EXB):

   "Then Jesus said to them, "So every teacher of the law (scribe) who has been taught about (become a disciple of) the kingdom of heaven is like the owner (head) of a house. He brings out both new things and old things he has saved (from his treasure / storeroom; knowledge of the Old Testament provides insight into Jesus' "new" message of the kingdom of God)."

8. Colossians 1:15; Hebrews 1:3

Day 8

1. Matthew 22:37-39
2. John 13:34 (CEV).
3. Greek - Strong's number G25
4. 1 John 4:8, 16
5. Romans 5:5
6. 1 John 4:19
7. Deuteronomy 10:16
8. Jeremiah 4:4
9. Jeremiah 31:31-33
10. Ezekiel 36:26-27
11. Romans 2:29; 6:6; Galatians 5:24; 2 Corinthians 5:17
12. Jeremiah 31:31-34; Luke 22:20
13. 1 John 4:19

Day 9

1. Luke 14:33 (AMPC)
2. Jeremiah 31:34; John 10:14
3. Jeremiah 23:18; John 10:3-4
4. John 14:26; 16:13; Psalm 25:14; 32:8
5. Proverbs 4:23
6. Proverbs 16:23; Matthew 12:34; James 3:8-10; Proverbs 18:21; Jeremiah 17:9
7. 1 John 4:8, 16
8. 1 Corinthians 13:5 (NIrV)
9. John 10:10
10. Romans 6:16-19
11. Matthew 10:39; 2 Corinthians 3:17; Galatians 5:1

Day 10

[1.] Luke 6:27-28
[2.] Luke 6:27-28 (NIrV)
[3.] Luke 6:35-36
[4.] Matthew 1:23; John 5:19; 5:36; 8:28; 10:25; 10:32; 10:37-38; 12:49; 14:7-11; 17:4; Colossians 1:15; Hebrews 1:3
[5.] Matthew 5:48; Luke 6:35; John 17:18
[6.] 1 John 4:4
[7.] Matthew 5:16; John 15:8
[8.] Romans 5:5
[9.] John 1:12-13; Romans 8:14-17; Galatians 4:4-7; 1 John 3:1
[10.] Ephesians 4:24; 1 John 4:17

Day 11

[1.] John 9:27-28
[2.] Exodus 31:18
[3.] Mark 10:18; Luke 18:19
[4.] Matthew 5:48
[5.] Romans 7:12
[6.] Romans 7:14-20
[7.] Romans 3:20
[8.] Romans 3:23
[9.] Deuteronomy 27:26; Galatians 3:10; James 2:10
[10.] Galatians 3:24
[11.] Romans 3:21-22; 5:17; 2 Corinthians 5:21
[12.] Romans 3:22
[13.] 2 Corinthians 3:7-9; Romans 6:14; 10:4
[14.] Romans 5:17
[15.] John 5:39-40; Romans 10:3; Matthew 5:17
[16.] Romans 3:22, 24
[17.] Galatians 3:1-5; 5:2-5
[18.] Galatians 5:1

Day 12

[1.] Mark 8:15 (GW)
[2.] Matthew 16:7
[3.] Matthew 16:11-12
[4.] Mark 8:15
[5.] Matthew 16:6
[6.] Matthew 16:12

7. Matthew15:7; 23:15, 23, 25, 27, 29; Mark 7:6; Luke 12:1
8. Matthew 23:27-28; Luke 11:39-41
9. Mark 7:6
10. Mark 7:7-8
11. Proverbs 4:20-22; Hebrews 4:12
12. Matthew 15:6, 14; 23:16-19; Mark 7:13; Luke 11:52
13. Matthew 15:3-6; Mark 7:9-13
14. Matthew 16:6
15. Matthew 15:1-9; 23:1-36; Mark 7:5-13; Luke 11:37-54
16. Matthew 13:33; Luke 13:20-21
17. Matthew 16:7-11; Mark 8:17-21

Day 13

1. Mark 6:31
2. Mark 6:31-33
3. Matthew 20:17-19; Luke 10:23; John 14, 15, 16
4. Mark 4:10-11, 33-34; Luke 9:18-21
5. Hebrews 13:8
6. Matthew 11:15; 13:9; Mark 4:9, 23; 7:16
7. Matthew 6:6; John 11:54
8. 1 Kings 19:11-13
9. Psalm 25:14
10. 1 Corinthians 2:7-12
11. Luke 11:13; 18:6-8; Hebrews 10:19-22; 1 John 5:14-15
12. Psalm 25:12; 32:8
13. Jeremiah 23:18, 22; 33:3
14. Proverbs 4:20-22; Hebrews 4:12; John 7:37-39
15. Proverbs 4:22 - Hebrew *'marpê'* - Strong's H4832
16. Proverbs 16:24; 24:13-14; Jeremiah 15:16; Ezekiel 3:1-3
17. Mark 6:31b (CEV).
18. Matthew 13:16-17; Luke 10:23-24; John 10:3-4
19. Psalm 18:39; 28:7; 73:26; 118:14; 138:3 as examples
20. Mark 6:31b (CEV)

Day 14

1. Matthew 7:15-23
2. Galatians 5:22-23
3. 1 John 4:8, 16; 1 Corinthians 13:4-7
4. Galatians 5:19-21
5. Romans 6:6; Galatians 5:24

6. 2 Corinthians 5:17
7. John 3:5-8; 1 Peter 1:23
8. Romans 8:29; 1 Corinthians 15:49; Colossians 3:10
9. Romans 8:13; Colossians 1:27
10. Romans 12:2; 2 Corinthians 3:18 (Greek *'metamorphóō'* - Strong's G3339),
11. 1 Corinthians 2:12; Galatians 4:6; 1 John 4:4
12. Matthew 5:16; John 15:8

Day 15

1. John 13:3-17
2. Genesis 1:1; Psalm 8:3; 89:11; 96:5; 102:25; 115:15; 121:2; 124:8; 134:3; 146:5-6
3. Psalm 147:4
4. Matthew 10:30
5. Psalm 111:2; 145:5
6. John 1:1-3, 14; Hebrews 2:14, 17; 4:15
7. Colossians 1:15-16
8. Romans 5:12
9. John 1:9-11; Matthew 16:21; Mark 8:31; 9:31
10. John 1:14
11. Mark 10:45
12. Mark 10:42-43 (NLT) - emphasis mine.
13. 1 Corinthians 2:16; Isaiah 55:9
14. Mark 10:43
15. 1 Corinthians 12:7

Day 16

1. John 14:27 (NIrV)
2. Isaiah 9:6-7
3. John 5:24; Colossians 1:13 - note tenses
4. Hebrews 2:14-15
5. John 16:33; Colossians 2:15; Hebrews 2:14-15; 1 John 3:8b
6. Matthew 28:18; Ephesians 1:20-23
7. Ephesians 2:6
8. John 14:17-20
9. Mark 11:23; James 4:7; 1 Peter 5:8-10
10. Matthew 10:1; Luke 9:1; 10:19; Psalm 91:13
11. Ephesians 6:17

Endnotes

Day 17

1. 2 Corinthians 2:15
2. 2 Corinthians 2:15-16 (NLT)
3. Romans 8:7-8
4. Mark 4:16-17
5. Acts 1:8b
6. Ephesians 6:12
7. 2 Corinthians 10:3-5; Ephesians 6:10-17
8. 2 Corinthians 10:4
9. Matthew 5:44
10. Philippians 2:9-11
11. Ephesians 6:17
12. Luke 11:9-10; Philippians 4:6-7
13. 2 Samuel 22:1-7; Psalm 18:1-3; Psalm 91
14. Isaiah 26:3; Philippians 4:7

Day 18

1. Luke 11:34 (TLB)
2. Proverbs 4:20-21
3. Proverbs 4:24
4. Proverbs 4:20-22; 12:14a; 12:18b; 15:4; 16:24
5. Matthew 6:22-23; Luke 11:34-36
6. Mark 4:24; Luke 8:18
7. Matthew 12:36-37

Day 19

1. *We know this man was already a follower of Jesus because he recognises the lordship of Jesus over his life - which is why he asked Jesus' permission. Jesus' reply also indicates he had already started to 'plough' with Him. - Luke 9:61-62*
2. Luke 9:61
3. Luke 9:62 (GW)
4. 1 Kings 19:19-21
5. Exodus 16:2-3; 17:1-3
6. Exodus 3:8; 3:17; 13:5; 33:1-3; Leviticus 20:24; Deut. 6:3; 8:7-10; 11:8-12
7. Joshua 5:4-7
8. Philippians 3:13 (WE)
9. 2 Corinthians 11:23-28
10. Philippians 3:14
11. Ephesians 1:18; 2 Timothy 1:8-9; 2 Peter 1:10
12. Colossians 3:1-2
13. John 15:8; Ephesians 2:10

Endnotes

Day 20

[1.] John 6:53-58
[2.] 2 Corinthians 5:21
[3.] Romans 6:6, 14, 17-18, 23; 8:2; Hebrews 2:14-15
[4.] Isaiah 53:4; Matthew 8:17; Galatians 3:13
[5.] Isaiah 53:4-5; Matthew 8:17; 1 Peter 2:24
[6.] Isaiah 54:10; Jeremiah 31:31; Matthew 26:28
[7.] Ephesians 1:18-20

Day 21

[1.] Matthew 24:29-30, 42; Mark 13:24-26, 32-33; Luke 21:25-28
[2.] Matthew 24:42, 44; Mark 13:33, 35-37; Luke 12:35-36
[3.] Matthew 24:1-31
[4.] Mark 13:1-8; Luke 21:5-28
[5.] Matthew 24:32-33; Mark 13:28-29; Luke 21:29-31
[6.] Matthew 24:45-51
[7.] Matthew 24:48-51
[8.] Matthew 25:1-13
[9.] Acts 4:31; 13:52; Ephesians 5:18; Philippians 1:11; Colossians 1:9
[10.] Luke 11:13
[11.] Matthew 25:14-30
[12.] Matthew 25:24-25
[13.] Matthew 25:31-46
[14.] Matthew 25:46
[15.] Romans 5:15-17; 2 Corinthians 5:21
[16.] Matthew 9:13; 25:34-40

Day 22

[1.] John 8:12; 9:5; 12:46
[2.] John 12:35-36; 1 Thessalonians 5:4-5; Galatians 3:28
[3.] John 14:18-20
[4.] Matthew 5:14
[5.] Psalm 24:1; 33:8; 46:10; 47:2; 48:10; 66:4; 67:7; Isaiah 9:6-7
[6.] Luke 13:16; John 10:10a; Acts 10:38
[7.] John 8:10-11
[8.] John 10:10b
[9.] Matthew 16:18-19; Revelation 3:20
[10.] Ephesians 2:10; Matthew 11:29-30; Luke 10:17
[11.] Matthew 5:14-15; Mark 4:21; Luke 11:33
[12.] Matthew 5:16

Endnotes

Day 23

1. Matthew 4:17; Luke 4:18-21; John 7:37-39
2. Matthew 22:9-10; 1 Timothy 2:3-4; 2 Peter 3:9
3. Matthew 10:7; Mark 16:15; Luke 9:2; 9:60
4. Isaiah 59:2; Colossians 2:13-14
5. Hebrews 4:16
6. Isaiah 61:10; Matthew 22:1-14
7. Matthew 22:4; Luke 14:16-17
8. Isaiah 55:1-3
9. Matthew 9:13; Colossians 1:13-14
10. Isaiah 53:4-5
11. Jeremiah 29:11
12. Luke 11:20
13. Acts 10:38
14. Matthew 10:7
15. 1 Peter 3:15
16. Matthew 10:8; Mark 16:17-18; Luke 9:1-2; 10:8-9

Day 24

1. *Luke 5:10 tells us that Simon Peter was in partnership with John and his brother James (sons of Zebedee). Mark 1:19-20 tells us that this partnership had 'hired servants' - they paid others to work for them.*
2. Matthew 4:18-20; Mark 10:28; Luke 18:28
3. Matthew 14:28-33
4. Mark 5:40; Luke 8:51
5. Matthew 17:1, 2-8
6. Matthew 26:57-58; Mark 14:53-54; Luke 22:54-55, 66
7. Matthew 26:69-70; Mark 14:66-68; Luke 22:55-57; John 18:17-18
8. Matthew 26:71-72; Mark 14:69-70; Luke 22:58; John 18:25
9. Matthew 26:73-74; Mark 14:70-71; Luke 22:59-60
10. Matthew 26:35; Mark 14:31
11. Matthew 26:75; Luke 22:62
12. Acts 2:14-41
13. Acts 3:1-10
14. Acts 5:15
15. Mark 16:7; John 21:1-2; 1 Corinthians 15:4-5
16. John 21:15-19
17. Acts 2:1-4; 4:8; 4:31; 13:52
18. Jeremiah 29:11; Ephesians 2:10

Endnotes

Day 25

1. Acts 1:4-8
2. John 14:12 & 16:7; 1 John 4:4
3. Colossians 2:15; Hebrews 2:14-15; 1 John 3:8b
4. Matthew 28:18-20
5. Matthew 5:16; John 15:8
6. Luke 13:10-13
7. Matthew 9:6-8; 15:31; Mark 2:11-12; Luke 5:24-26; 7:15-16; 17:12-16; John 11:4; Acts 4:21
8. Matthew 10:1,7-8; Mark 16:15-18; Luke 9:1-2
9. Luke 13:11; Acts 10:38
10. Isaiah 9:6-7; Luke 11:20
11. 1 Corinthians 1:26-31
12. Matthew 11:11; 2 Corinthians 5:17
13. John 3:5-8; 1 Peter 1:23; 1 John 3:9
14. 1 John 4:4
15. Romans 8:19-21

Day 26

1. Romans 8:29; 12:2; 2 Corinthians 3:18; Ephesians 4:22-24; Colossians 3:10
2. Matthew 10:24-25a
3. Matthew 13:54; Mark 6:2
4. Matthew 9:36; 14:14; 15:32; 20:34; Mark 1:41; 6:34; 8:2; Luke 7:13
5. Matthew 9:13; 9:27; 15:22; 17:15; 20:30-31; Mark 10:47-48; Luke 1:68-79; 17:13
6. Greek for compassion = *'splanchnizomai'* (Strong's G4697) - literally means *'to have the bowels yearn'*
7. Colossians 1:15; Hebrews 1:3
8. Galatians 5:22-23
9. Romans 6:21-23
10. Deuteronomy 30:19-20; John 10:10

Day 27

1. John 14:12a (GW)
2. Luke 4:18 (GW)
3. Matthew 9:2-7; Luke 1:77; 7:47-50
4. Luke 4:18-19
5. Luke 11:20
6. Matthew 10:1, 7-8; Mark 3:14-15; 16:15-18; Luke 9:1-2; 10:1, 17-20; 24:45-49; John 20:21-23

7. Hebrews 13:8
8. Luke 24:47; John 20:23
9. Galatians 4:6
10. Matthew 1:23
11. John 3:34
12. John 17:18; 20:21
13. Luke 24:49; Acts 1:4-5
14. 1 Peter 3:15
15. Zechariah 4:6; 1 Corinthians 3:6-7

Day 28

1. Matthew 8:1-4
2. Matthew 8:5-13
3. Matthew 8:14-15
4. Matthew 8:16-17
5. Matthew 8:28-33
6. Matthew 9:1-8
7. Matthew 9:20-22
8. Matthew 9:32-33
9. Matthew 9:18-19, 23-31
10. Matthew 9:35
11. Matthew 9:37-38 (NIrV).
12. Matthew 10:1
13. John 4:35 (NLT).
14. Matthew 9:36
15. Matthew 10:8
16. Matthew 10:1

Day 29

1. *The disciples were with Jesus at the wedding in Cana where He performed His first miracle - John 2:1-2, 11-12*
2. Matthew 4:18-22; Mark 2:14; John 1:43
3. Matthew 28:19; Mark 16:15; Luke 24:47
4. Mark 16:17, 20; Acts 4:29-30; 14:3; Romans 15:18-19
5. John 14:12
6. Luke 10:17-19
7. Matthew 14:19; 15:36; Mark 8:6; Luke 9:16
8. Acts 2:43; 4:30; 5:12-16; 8:13; 14:3
9. Matthew 28:19
10. Romans 15:18-19

Endnotes

Day 30

[1] Matthew 28:20a
[2] John 14:12; 1 John 2:6
[3] John 10:10
[4] Isaiah 9:6-7; Matthew 28:19a
[5] Matthew 9:38

'Defeating Fear, Panic, and Anxiety'

- A 30-day devotional

Fear, panic, and anxiety are real and debilitating forces that hold people back from reaching their full potential in life. Jesus came to set us free from these bondages so that we could experience life as God intended it to be. This 30-day devotional looks at what Christ has done to set us free, as well as explaining what the individual's response should be so they can move into the freedom that God promises those who put their faith in Jesus. An essential read for anybody who is struggling with an oppression of any description.

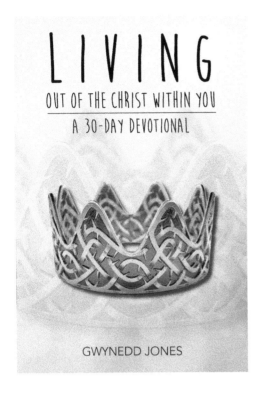

'Living Out of The Christ Within You'

- A 30-day devotional

What it means to be a *'new creation'* in Christ is one of the least taught subjects from the Bible, yet for the Christian it is one of the most important. *'Living Out of The Christ Within You'* is a 30-day devotional that helps bring clarity regarding the spiritual identity of the individual who has put their faith in Jesus Christ. It is as we begin to understand our new identity that we become better equipped to re-present Jesus to the world around us.